Just
Packards

MAGNIFICENT MACHINES & TIMELESS CLASSICS

Published by

Krause Publications, a division of F+W Media, Inc.
700 East State Street • Iola, WI 54990-0001
715-445-2214 • 888-457-2873
www.krausebooks.com

To order books or other products call toll-free 1-800-258-0929
or visit us online at www.krausebooks.com or www.Shop.Collect.com

Library of Congress Control Number: 2010925547

ISBN-13: 978-1-4402-1427-1
ISBN-10: 1-4402-1427-1

Designed by Sharon Bartsch
Edited by Brian Earnest

Printed in the United States of America

CONTENTS

"**P**ackard was THE car!" Pat Hume told me years ago in an interview. She was one of the last Packard regional distribution officials around. Pat was well into her 80s but her eyes sparkled like a child's at the very mention of the name Packard. She had spent much of her working life with the marque from about 1930 to 1954, dedicating her career to the brand she KNEW was the best.

She was not alone. More than 1.6 million new Packards were sold from 1899 until the marque's final model rolled off the assembly line in the 1950s. Today, Packard remains one of the most collected and proudly owned cars in America — and still enjoys prestige status overseas.

Generally, Packards were made to run well, were comfortable, and carried exclusive styling enhanced by quality appointments. It was a conservative car in many respects. It was the car of choice that dominated at high-society gatherings, major business events, and important political conventions. Yet, even away from fancy settings, a Packard bespoke its lineage.

Packard put its mystique into words in 1936: "Only a few jewels achieve the rare distinction of being 'solitaires.' For only a few can appear magnificent without a flattering setting. The Packard, we feel, is one of these jewels. Even if you take away its proud name, even if you strip it of its enduring identity – it will still be a monarch among motor cars. It will still be without a peer in mechanical excellence. It will still be without an equal in the luxury men and women love.

"But you can no more divorce a Packard from its name, from its prestige and identity, than you can separate it from its comfort, or the swift-flowing ease with which it rides the roads. For... the Packard name has stood for the utmost in fine motor cars...Packard ownership has been a symbol of success."

Pat knew that. So did the other 1.6 million owners. Whether their models were prestigious Twin Sixes or Twelves, Custom Super Eights or even the lesser priced sixes and eight-cylinder One Twenty, the Packard heritage was embodied in every bolt and stitch. If you really want to know what that meant then – and now – simply "Ask the Man Who Owns One."

"ASK THE MAN WHO OWNS ONE"

PACKARD BY THE NUMBERS

Making heads and tails of Packard series numbers

The 1923 Fleetwood-bodied Twin Six phaeton.

Like most carmakers, Packard developed a number of ways to identify and market its fine automobiles. Today, if you ask the man who owns one just what type of Packard he has, his answer may be a bit confusing. He may say, "it's a 1932 Twin Six," or he could reply that his car is simply "a Series 905." Both of his replies would be correct, but a true Packard fan of the Classic era might be the only person, besides the owner, who would be so well in tune.

Packard began the great run of series starting in 1921 with the "First" series of the Single Six models. In 1924, when the Single Eight was launched, this line began with its own "First" series, and this is the number base that Packard would use for many more years.

There were a number of changes as to how the Series numbers were applied over the years of Packard's life. The following gives a basic run down of Packard Series numbers. Applications were often dependent on engine, body trim levels and wheelbase lengths.

From the start in 1921 to the early 1930s, Series numbers such as 626 or 745 would often represent the wheelbases of these cars. Later, arbitrary numbers were applied, and usually the higher the last number, the larger the engine or higher degree of trim level applied.

In the following list, the marketing or model names are in quotation marks, followed by the Series applied to individual models.

1923 Packard First Series, Single Six

1924 Packard First Series, Single Eight

1921-1922 (1st Series)
"Single Six, First Series"
Series No. 116

1923 (1st Series)
"Single Six, First Series"
Series No. 126, 133

1924 (1st/2nd Series)
"Single Eight, First Series"
Series No. 136, 143
"Single Six, Second Series"
Series No. 226, 233

1925-1926 (2nd/3rd Series)
"Second Series, Eight"
Series No. 236, 243
"Third Series, Six"
Series No. 326, 333

1927 (3rd/4th Series)
"Third Series, Eight"
Series No. 336, 343
"Fourth Series, Six"
Series No. 426, 433

1928 (4th/5th Series)
"Fourth Series, Eight"

1925 Packard Second Series, Eight

(Custom and Standard)
Series No. 443
"Fifth Series, Six"
Series No. 526, 533

1929 (6th Series)
"Standard Eight, Sixth Series"
Series No. 626, 633
"Speedster, Sixth Series"
Series No. 626
"Custom Eight, Sixth Series"
Series No. 640
"Deluxe Eight, Sixth Series"
Series No. 645

1930 (7th Series)
"Standard Eight, Seventh Series"
Series No. 726, 733
"Speedster, Seventh Series"

Series No. 734
"Custom Eight, Seventh Series"
Series No. 740
"Deluxe Eight, Seventh Series"
Series No. 745

1931 (8th Series)
"Standard Eight, Eighth Series"
Series No. 826, 833
"Individual Custom Eight, Eighth Series"
Series No. 833, 840
"Deluxe Series, Eighth Series"
Series No. 840, 845

1932 (9th Series)
"Ninth Series, Light Eight"
Series 900
"Ninth Series, Standard Eight"
Series 901, 902

"Ninth Series, Deluxe Eight"
(also "Individual Eight," 904 only)
Series 903, 904
"Ninth Series, Twin Six" (V-12)
Series 905

1933 (10th Series)
"Tenth Series, Eight"
Series 1001, 1002
"Tenth Series, Super Eight"
Series 1003, 1004
"Tenth Series, Twelve"
Series 1005, 1006

1934 (11th Series)
"Eleventh Series, Eight"
Series No. 1100, 1101, 1102
"Eleventh Series, Super Eight"
Series No. 1103, 1104, 1105
"Eleventh Series, Twelve"
Series No. 1106, 1107, 1108

1935 (12th Series)
"Twelfth Series, One Twenty"
Series No. None
"Twelfth Series, Eight"
Series No. 1200, 1201, 1202
"Twelfth Series, Super Eight"
Series No. 1203, 1204, 1205
"Twelfth Series, Twelve"
Series No. 1206, 1207, 1208

1936 (14th Series)
"Fourteenth Series, One Twenty"
Series No. 120-B
"Fourteenth Series, Eight"

1926 Packard Third Series, Six

1928 Fifth Series, Six

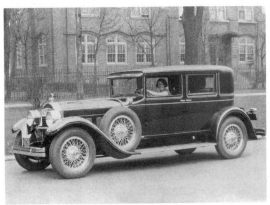

1928 Fourth Series, Eight

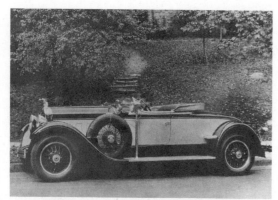
1929 Packard Sixth Series, Deluxe Eight

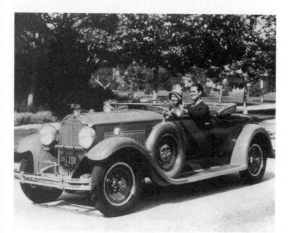
1930 Packard Seventh Series, Standard Eight

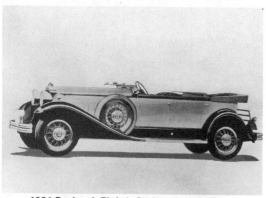
1931 Packard, Eighth Series, Deluxe Eight

Series No. 1400, 1401, 1402
"Fourteenth Series, Super Eight"
Series No. 1403, 1404, 1405
"Fourteenth Series, Twelve"
Series No. 1406, 1407, 1408

1937 (15th Series)
"Fifteenth Series, Six"
Series No. 115-C
"Fifteenth Series, One Twenty"
Series No. 120-D, 120-CD, 138-CD
"Fifteenth Series, Super Eight"
Series No. 1500, 1501, 1502
"Fifteenth Series, Twelve"
Series No. 1506, 1507, 1508

1938 (16th Series)
"Sixteenth Series, Six"
Series No. 1600
"Sixteenth Series, Eight"
(formerly the One Twenty models)
Series no. 1601, 1601-D, 1602
"Sixteenth Series, Super Eight"
Series No. 1603, 1604, 1605
"Sixteenth Series, Twelve"
Series No. 1606, 1607, 1608

1939 (17th Series)
"Seventeenth Series, Six"
Series No. 1700
"Seventeenth Series, One Twenty"
Series No. 1701, 1702
"Seventeenth Series, Super Eight"
Series No. 1703, 1705
"Seventeenth Series, Twelve"
Series No. 1707, 1708

1940 (18th Series)

"Eighteenth Series, One Ten" (Six)
Series No. 1800
"Eighteenth Series, One Twenty"
Series No. 1801
"Eighteenth Series, One Sixty"
(aka Super Eight)
Series No. 1803, 1804, 1805
Eighteenth Series, One Eighty"
(aka Custom-Eight)
Series No. 1806, 1807, 1808

1932 Packard Ninth Series, Light Eight

1941 (19th Series)

"Nineteenth Series, One Ten" (Six)
Series No. 1900
"Nineteenth Series, One Twenty"
Series No. 1901
"Nineteenth Series, One Sixty"
(Super Eight)
Series No. 1903, 1904, 1905
"Nineteenth Series, One Eighty"
(Custom Eight)
Series No. 1906, 1907, 1908
"Nineteenth Series, Clipper"
Series No. 1951

1933 Packard Tenth Series, Twelve

1942 (20th Series)

"Twentieth Series, Six"
Series No. 2000, 2010, 2020, 2030
"Twentieth Series, Eight"
Series No. 2001, 2011, 2021
"Twentieth Series, One Sixty"
(aka Super Eight)
Series No. 2003, 2004, 2005, 2023,
  2055

1934 Packard, Eleventh Series, Eight

1935 Packard Twelfth Series, One-Twenty

1936 Packard Fourteenth Series, Twelve

1937 Packard Fifteenth Series, Twelve

1938 Packard Sixteenth Series, Twelve

"Twentieth Series, One Eighty"
(Custom Eight)
Series No. 2006, 2007, 2008

1946-1947 (21st series)
"Clipper Six"
Series No. 2100
"Clipper Standard Eight"
Series No. 2101
"Clipper Deluxe Eight"
Series No. 2111
"Super Clipper Eight"
Series No. 2103
"Custom Super Clipper Eight"
Series No. 2106, 2126

1948-1949 (22nd Series)
"Standard Eight"
Series No. 2201
"Deluxe Eight"
Series No. 2211
"Super Eight"
Series No. 2202, 2222, 2232
"Custom Eight"
Series No. 2203, 2226, 2233

1949 (23rd Series)
"Standard Eight" and "Deluxe Eight"
Series No. 2301
 "Super Eight" and "Super Deluxe
    Eight"
Series No. 2302, 2322, 2332
"Custom Eight"
Series No. 2306, 2333

1950 (23rd Series)

"Standard Eight" & "Deluxe Eight"
Series No. 2301-5
"Super Eight" & "Super Deluxe
 Eight"
Series No. 2302-5, 2322-5, 2332-5
"Custom Eight"
Series No. 2306-5, 2333-5

1951 (24th Series)

"Packard 200" (Standard & Deluxe)
"Packard 250"
Series No. 2401
"Packard 300"
Series No. 2402
"Patrician 400"
Series No. 2406

1952 (25th Series)

"Packard 200" (Standard & Deluxe)
Series No. 2501
"Packard 250"
Series No. 2531
"Packard 300"
Series No. 2502
"Patrician 400"
Series No. 2506

1953 (26th Series)

"Clipper Special"
Series No. 2601
"Clipper Deluxe"
Series No. 2611
"Cavalier"
Series No. 2602, 2631
(Mayfair hardtop & Cavalier conv.)

1939 Packard Seventeenth Series, Six

**1940 Packard Eighteenth Series, One-Eighty
(Custom Eight)**

1941 Packard Nineteenth Series, One-Ten (Six)

**1942 Packard Twentieth Series, One-Sixty
(Super Eight)**

1948 Packard Twenty-Second Series, Standard Eight

1946 Packard Twenty-First Series,
Custom Super Clipper Eight

1950 Packard Twenty-Third Series,
Super Deluxe Eight

"Caribbean"
Series No. 2631
"Patrician"
Series No. 2606
Corporate Executive
(Henney eight-passenger sedans
 and limousines)
Series No. 2626

1954 (54th Series)

"Deluxe"
Series No. 5401
"Super" & "Panama"
Series No. 5411
"Cavalier"
Series No. 5402
"Pacific" & "Caribbean"
(includes standard Packard
 convertible)
Series No. 5431

1955 (55th Series)
"Clipper Deluxe," "Clipper Super"
  & "Panama Super"
Series No. 5540
"Clipper Custom" & "Clipper
Constellation"
Series No. 5560
"Four Hundred," "Patrician" &
  "Caribbean"
Series No. 5580

1956 (56th series)
"Clipper Deluxe," Clipper Super"
  & "Panama Super"
Series No. 5640
"Clipper Custom" & "Clipper
Constellation"
Series No. 5660
"Executive"
Series No. 5670
"Four Hundred" & "Patrician"
Series No. 5680
"Caribbean"
Series No. 5688

1957
"Clipper"
Series No. 57L

1958
"Clipper"
Series No. 58L
"Hawk"
Series No. 58LS

1951 Packard Twenty-Fourth Series, Patrician 400

1952 Packard Twenty-Fifth Series, Packard 250

**1953 Packard Twenty-Sixth Series,
Patrician Formal Sedan**

**1954 Packard Fifty-Fourth Series,
Caribbean**

1955 Packard Fifty-Fifth Series, Clipper Custom

1956 Packard Fifty-Sixth Series, Four Hundred

1957 Packard, Clipper

1958 Packard, Clipper

THE CYLINDER WAR

With the Twin Six, Packard believed more lungs were better

With the smooth-running performance of the glorious Twin Six engine beating in a 1915 touring car like this Packard ruled the luxury car market and gained global importance.

"From the time when the first practical car made its first run on the road, there have been three things which every motorist has asked for — more range of ability, greater smoothness and less noise," assessed Jesse Vincent, chief engineer of the Packard Motor Car Co. and, by reason of that high honor, a vice president of the same.

His words came midyear in 1915 as his company turned a mighty significant corner in automobile production. Packard had introduced the world to the Twin Six, the first successful, American-made 12-cylinder engine. The invention, spearheaded, by

the genius of Vincent, rocked the industrial sector, made Wall Street take notice and sent a wave of anticipation through the car business. Cadillac, which had pioneered the V-8 engine configuration, had cast its lot on that fresh design. Now its innovation was being one-upped by Packard. So it was in the automobile business.

Vincent knew the rise of multi-cylinder configurations was a progression from single cylinder to twin, to the four, then the six and next the eight. But the 12 was novel, a mystical blend of speed and luxury beating in the chest of a Packard. Beating softly, gently, in perfect rhythm, soothing the driver, assuring passengers and being venerated by the public.

Vincent explained, "For a long time the six-cylinder motor seemed to fill the bill... but gradually reasons were discovered which made it seem advisable to split up the driving force.... A six-cylinder motor is theoretically in absolutely perfect balance, because the vibratory forces due to the rise and fall of one piston are neutralized by equal and opposite forces.... The pistons form what mathematicians call a 'system of bodies' and the forces existing in each individually have no effect on the whole lot...because of the cancelling...."

Sounded technical — and it was. But industrialists and engineers in the car realm ate it up. Good food for conversation. A wellspring of knowledge which could sow seeds for future innovations. That was Vincent. That was Packard, too, in 1915, mainly on the strength of its Twin Six.

There was mechanical danger in trying to coax too much power from a six. Vincent noted the extreme explosive effort it took to push a large, heavy cylinder down. The greater the force due to the enlargement of the cylinder, the greater the twist on the crankshaft. Bad scene. Pending breakdown.

He opted for less piston weight and smaller explosions. Good idea, and it worked. It was the innovation that made the Twin Six successful. It also resulted in less weight for pistons, crankcases and flywheels. Brilliant, indeed, and it led car makers to move toward a series of "light" cars, built with less material but providing the power, space, comfort and performance the public demanded.

"Light pistons and connecting rods allow the engine to have a greater range of speed, while the smaller bore of the cylinders permits the use of higher compression... [with] more efficient burning of the gas at all speeds." He added, "It seems obvious that the V or twin type is bound to be the best arrangement, as it allows the use of a short, stiff crankshaft, short, light, stiff motor and... the shortest possible wheelbase."

Notice how the term V-8 was not used? It must have stuck in Vincent's throat, perhaps from an engineering perspective, or because competitor Cadillac was first to efficiently manufacture and then market such an engine. He conceded that the "twin four" was "probably a little better than the six at moderate speeds, but at higher engine speeds, the advantage would switch to the six-cylinder motor as the unbalanced inertia forces become a very important factor... vibration would be a great deal more pronounced than in the six."

Lauding the virtues of the six, Vincent stated that the perfect balance of that configuration would be accentuated if two sixes were designed, one bank opposite the other, making it "in absolute theoretical and practical balance." He then told one of his secrets: "In designing this Twin Six motor, however, it is necessary to set the cylinders at an included angle of 60 instead of 20 degrees, as there will be six impulses per crankshaft revolution instead of four, and a circle divided into six parts gives 60 degrees."

What resulted was 50 percent better torque versus a twin four and 100 percent better than a six. The weight of the Twin Six was "a standoff" with the twin four, but lighter than the six. The Twin Six "is absolutely smooth at all speeds," Vincent said. Accessibility was better than the eight, due to the degree of banking: 90 degrees for the eight, 60 for the Twin Six. This allowed close placement of major components, such as the generator, water pump and starter.

Vincent had tossed down the gauntlet, and the multi-cylinder race was on. Some makers lined up to use V-8s of their own designs, others followed the twelve. Well into 1923, the Twin Six remained the engine of choice for Packard. The idea disappeared for less than a decade. A new version of the Twin Six was available to the public in 1932. It was soon renamed the Packard Twelve, and it ran through 1939.

And Vincent was still the genius behind the re-invention.

We need more men like him.

To read more about great Packards and the history of the company, check out the book Packard: An American Classic, by Richard Luckin, available at www.shopoldcarsweekly.com.

A $35,000 CAR – IN 1921

Editors Note: This story originally appeared in the August 1921 issue of *American Automobile Digest*. If you can add to the history or fate of this Packard, send an e-mail to oldcars@krause.com.

"**A**n automobile fortress that is at the same time one of the most luxurious limousines ever built has just been delivered to his excellency Tsan Tso-Lin, the Governor General of Manchuria. The machine, which in appearance and fact is the last word in luxurious transportation, is also an armored car, bullet and bomb-proof, and prepared either for offense or defense. The car has been especially manufactured on General Tsan's orders by the Packard Motors Export Corporation. It is likely to be a model for similar cars for other nervous rulers now that news of its construction is no longer a secret.

When General Tsan appears in the streets of Mukden or other Manchurian cities, he will apparently be traveling simply in an amazingly luxurious Packard Twin-Six limousine. The car has disteel wheels, special headlights, and is of a deep tan color with mahogany top and trimmings. Inside the fittings and finish are fully worthy of the official position of the great Governor General. To conform to the colors of Chinese royalty, the cushions, seat backs and arms are upholstered in purple and gold mohair. The panels lining the body are entirely of inlaid mahogany, and there are vanity cases of the same material on either side. The fittings and all metal used in the tonneau are of silver and cloissonne. Perhaps the most beautiful part of the interior decoration is the flowered marquetry inlaid in the door panels. In each of these panels more than 20 different kinds of wood are used.

This is the car as it appears to the eye. But if an attempt is made by some assassin to end General Tsan's term of office with a bullet, as is so frequently the fate of Chinese officials, the car can be transformed in a twinkling. Down from inside the roof come steel shutters, covering all the windows and reaching to the steel plates built inside the walls of the car. Concealed loopholes open on each side and in the rear and six automatics or rifles can come into action. Another steel shutter rises out of the partition between the tonneau and the driver's seat, closing off danger from the front. A Colt machine gun appears from under the driver's seat and is fastened onto a special bracket built in at the right-hand side of the cowling. The luxurious car is thus turned into a fortress.

As an additional measure of safety in dangerous times, there are fastened to each side of the car three swivels. Belts are provided that fasten into these with a snap-hook, so that soldiers may be strapped to the running-board and have both hands free to use rifles. Handles have been attached to the steel roof of the car for their convenience. So if attacked the car can in a moment become a bullet-proof steel box, defended by a machine gun and six soldiers on the outside and by six more rifles from the inside.

A few of the structural features of the car are of interest. In order to make it possible to conceal the chrome nickel steel shutters in the roof they were made of plates cut into strips and fastened by means of flexible steel bands. These run on roller bearings in

The panels are of inlaid mahogany. In each panel more than 20 different kinds of wood are used. The upholstery is in purple and gold mohair.

grooves in the window-sills. Each weighs approximately 75 pounds, and the problem of operating them was solved by installing a sprocket and chain devise built into the top of the car and operated by metal handles, which can easily be detached and stored in the partition pockets.

The great weight of the car, with the armored plate, machine gun and large number of passengers to be carried, called for unusual strength. The whole frame of the vehicle was heavily reinforced; the running-boards were strengthened; extra leaves were added to the springs, and Westinghouse air springs were attached. All windows were constructed of triplex glass, especially constructed to prevent splintering when hit by bullets.

Story and photos by Angelo Van Bogart

FROM PARTS TO PACKARD
Dedicated hobbyists revives Fleetwood-bodied 1924 Packard town car

Although this 1924 Packard Fleetwood-bodied town car probably has just 4,500 miles, it's led an eventful life. It went from a ritzy cabriolet to being cut up for use as a truck to a show beauty.

Don Hanson is among the old car hobby's bravest souls. When he found his 1924 Packard, a First Series Eight Fleetwood town car, it was more Packard than Fleetwood. The project was basically a combination between an incomplete 10,001-piece puzzle and a scavenger hunt to find missing parts. However, Hanson wasn't deterred one iota by the car's incomplete and rusty condition when he bought it in 1978.

"I wasn't disappointed, because I didn't know any better," Hanson said. "I had always wanted an early Packard, and for what [restored cars] were selling for, even then, it was more than I felt I could afford. So I was delighted with it."

Hanson was actually lucky to obtain the car. When he responded to the ad listing the Packard, he was told it had already been sold. Regardless, he left his phone num-

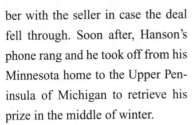

Above, the Packard as owner Don Hanson found it. The car was missing its body from the back doors rearward. Right, the first step to resurrecting the body was building new wood.

ber with the seller in case the deal fell through. Soon after, Hanson's phone rang and he took off from his Minnesota home to the Upper Peninsula of Michigan to retrieve his prize in the middle of winter.

"Basically, the chassis was complete, but the back half of the body had been cut off to make a truck out of it," Hanson said. "That was often done years ago, after the original owners discarded cars that had lost their usefulness."

When Hanson came upon the car, it was in a state similar to what Packard delivered to Fleetwood for coachwork. The chassis was complete and the car still carried the radiator, hood, front fenders and instrument panel. Fleetwood's aluminum cowl, front doors and partition between the chauffeur's compartment and rear cabin were also present. However, the rear doors, roof and back portion of the body were lost when a former owner started to make a truck in the 1950s.

"The guy I bought it from lived in Stam-

baugh, Michigan, and he bought it from the caretaker of the man who originally owned it," Hanson said. "[The seller] just decided it was too ambitious of a project and he threw in the towel.

"Really, it was almost a one-owner car. The original owner, Mr. Richey, was from Chicago," said Hanson, adding Richey was a president and board chairman of the Chicago Northwestern Railway. "He had a cabin in northern Wisconsin and he took it up there and it was up there its entire life. He died early in the 1950s and willed it to his caretaker, Otto Leino, and his name was painted on the door when I got it.

"I was told it was probably in good shape up until the 1950s, when Otto got it and tore the body off [before he returned to his native Norway] and it sat outside."

The owner had a "Daphne at the well" radiator cap from a later Packard fashioned for the car.

The instrument panel continues two-tone green paint inside. Gauges include fuel level, oil pressure, amperes, clock and a speedometer.

Despite missing part of its body, the custom-built car had many unique features still intact. In a nod to his railroad career, the original owner specified a red lamp on the driver's side running board splash shield and a green lamp on the passenger side. Hanson could also tell the car had originally been painted the same dark green color on the fenders as the body — an atypical feature since most Packards of this year had black fenders. The car also has sidemounts, which Packard did not offer in 1924, and the original wheels are optional 20-inch units, rather than the standard 21-inch wheels.

Such custom features only add to the obstacles in a restoration, so Hanson hoped he could find another Fleetwood-bodied 1924 Packard to help restore his car. He was not so lucky.

"I did find late-1920s and earlier than 1924 Fleetwoods," he said. "It would have been helpful if I could have located other 1924 Fleetwood-bodied Packards in restoring this car, but I never found any."

The Fleetwood Metal Body Co. was one of many coachbuilders that added to Packard's own already-extensive line of body styles in 1924. The Pennsylvania coachbuilder also supplied bodies to other makes of cars, but Packard was one of, if not Fleetwood's largest, customers at the time. It was founded in 1909 in a town of the same name where it built body styles of every configuration, from coupe to sedan to touring to limousine to cabriolet (town car), among others. As was the case with other

The 1924 Packard Fleetwood-bodied rides on the First Series, Single Eight chassis and has Fleetwood Style No. 2645 coachwork.

coachbuilders, Fleetwood bodies were built in runs or as an individual and unrepeated design, and could be trimmed to fit a customer's wishes or whims.

In 1925, Fleetwood Metal Body Co.'s shareholders sold out to Fisher Body Co., of which General Motors had a controlling stock share since 1919. In 1926, GM took complete control of Fisher in a stock exchange that gave it 100 percent of Fisher's shares. With that trade, Fleetwood Metal Body Co. was completely enveloped into GM, yet Fleetwood continued to produce bodies for other makes of chassis. Soon, General Motors built a satellite plant to Fleetwood in Detroit, then in 1930, all coachwork under the Fleetwood name was completed in Detroit while the Fleetwood, Pa., plant closed.

Despite the number that were built, Fleetwood-bodied Packard survivors appear to be rare, and with the rear section missing, and another Packard project car in the works, Hanson let the 1924 town car project languish as work on another Packard was completed. But he didn't stop thinking about the car. He placed advertisements annually in *Old Cars Weekly* and *Hemmings* in search of a rear section to the body, but those ads produced little results.

Regardless, he never considered parting with the daunting project. "I really didn't consider selling it, but often times I would contemplate finding another body when I didn't get a response to my ads," Hanson said. "The front section was all complete. Oherwise, I probably would have never attempted it. I thought all I had to do was find the rear tub section and doors, but the job proved to be difficult."

Underneath the body, the chassis remained complete and very restorable.

"It was explained to me that it only had 4,500 miles, which was on the odometer, but the glass [on the gauge] was broken and rusty because it had been sitting outside," he said. "While I wanted to believe that was true, I have no idea of knowing that. The frame and chassis were all intact and it looked very good. It looked complete and not messed with. But it was so rusty, the restoration work was considerable."

Despite its rust, the chassis was a good foundation with which to work. However, Hanson was still missing the rear section, so he began researching how the body should appear. He visited the Detroit Public Library and viewed historic images of similar vehicles, but his big break came in 1988 when he visited Phelps, Wis., the former home of Otto Leino and the vacation home of the Packard's original purchaser.

"I went to back where Otto lived, but first, I had to find out exactly where he lived, so I went to the postmaster in that town," Hanson said. "I asked where Otto Leino lived and found the property was pretty much abandoned. I had driven that far, so I looked around and found the rear section [buried in the dirt]. I only found the bottom half, but I was ecstatic because now I knew the configuration."

Shortly after, another piece fell into place.

"I received a response from an earlier *Old Cars Weekly* ad by an attorney living in Clintonville, Wis.," Hanson said. "He said he had a bunch of rear parts and sections that I could have, just come and get them! I didn't

This car sports optional 20-in. wheels, all of which have Fleetwood body No. 7577 stamped on them. This number can also be found on the windshield, bolts, sidemount hardware and other parts.

Jumps seats come out of the division between the driver and passenger compartment.

take a trailer because I didn't expect to get anything. In the basement of his law office, he had a 1929 or '30 Packard and he had all kinds of parts. He gave me two top rear sections. I didn't know which one I could use, if

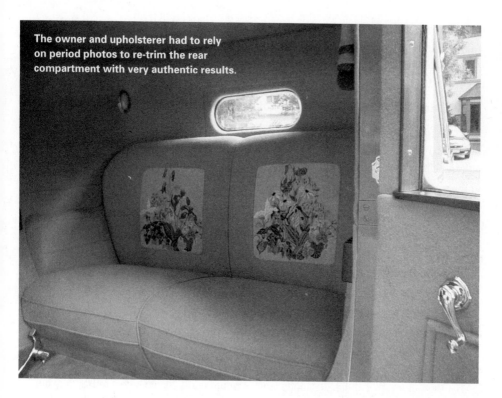
The owner and upholsterer had to rely on period photos to re-trim the rear compartment with very authentic results.

any, but I managed to get them in the trunk of my car and dragged them home."

An ad did result in the purchase of a sedan body, which provided the rear doors and some small parts. Hanson then delivered the town car's body parts to Gene Irvine of New Madison, Ohio, to have all new wood fabricated for the town car body. In 1997, the body and its new wood frame work were returned to Hanson for the fitting of the body panels, which proved challenging.

Over that winter, Hanson mounted the town car body on the donor car's frame so he could work on the original chassis and the body at the same time. The chassis was cleaned and he prepared to start the engine in the spring.

"Using a beer case for a seat, I towed the car for initial start up," he said. "It fired almost immediately, and within minutes it was running quite well. I drove the chassis, with the beer case seat, around the neighborhood for several trips. The engine ran smoothly, no leaks, no noise from within and no smoke. The engine is also equipped with an air compressor that runs off the transmission — gotta pump up the tires, you know! — [and] it also worked perfectly when engaged.

"I still haven't rebuilt the engine and it runs extremely well."

Hanson took the cleaned chassis to Odyssey Restorations in Spring Lake Park, Minn., to be fully restored. The craftsmen at

Odyssey Restorations completed mechanical work and dealt with the chassis rust. In the mean time, Hanson continued fitting the body metal, and when it was completed in 2003, he took it to Wayne Kempfert of Minneapolis for paint. Hanson chose a light green in place of the original dark green, and its lighter hue has become an attention grabber.

"I was after elegance, and I was after something more bright and cheerful," he said. "I considered gray, but decided on two shades of contrasting green. A great deal of time was spent sorting out different samples of paint before coming up with the acceptable combination. The color combination is usually the first thing that people comment on — they like it."

By the summer of 2004, the body and sorted-out chassis had been reunited and the Packard was ready to be trimmed. Hanson selected to Rick Tillman of R&R Upholstery in White Bear Lake, Minn., to install the roof over the rear compartment. Admittedly, Hanson was particular on how the top should look to remain authentic, but he was pleased with Tillman's work and hired him to upholster the inside. Left with little clue how the interior originally looked, Hanson and Tillman relied on period photos uncovered in the Detroit Public Library's collection and other Packard publications.

Meanwhile, the 85-hp, 357.8-cid straight-eight's water jackets leaked and the engine registered low oil pressure, so with the prodding of a fellow Packard enthusiast, Hanson continued to tweak the engine. He now knows his car's engine front to back and how to properly tune it.

"I should have put zippers on the oil pan and front cover, I had them off and on so many times," he said.

In late 2009, the car was ready to be shown, and it made its first appearance at the Meadow Brook Concours d'Elegance, followed by the Salisbury Concours d'Elegance. In 2010, the Packard was shown at two Classic Car Club of America meets, where its received its Primary and Senior Awards. Hanson also hopes to enter the car in Antique Automobile Club of America events in the near future.

"The Packard has been well received, which is very gratifying," Hanson said. "I would really like to take it to Hershey in October and that's a big commitment," he said. "When I took it to the Masterpiece, I got the Most Elegant Award. The Packard always receives some kind of award. It's nice to get an award, but I enjoy the show for the show. Talking to people about the car and cars is really an enjoyable experience."

Through the years, Hanson has sold cars in order to start new projects, but this Packard might just be a keeper.

"I would like to think I won't sell it, but we're all just caretakers," he said. "It's the journey — not the destination — that drives us."

Maybe there is another Packard puzzle waiting around the corner. And if there is, Hanson is just the man to put it back together.

The 1924 Packard First Series Single Eight

In Packard history, 1924 is a big year. It's the first year the company established the famous numeric series that would be used until the last Packard of 1958. 1924 also marked the first use of four-wheel brakes on a Packard, and the introduction of the straight-eight, which served as a worthy replacement to the fabulous Twin Six.

Packard offered two lines in 1924: the First Series Single Eight and the Second Series Single Six. (The First Series Single Six designation dates to 1921, but was interrupted by the introduction of the First Series Single Eight straight-eight 1924 model from which the series designations commenced until a 1953 interruption.)

The Single Eight model was introduced June 14, 1923, and carried 136 and 143 model designations to reflect the two available wheelbase lengths, which were ten inches longer than the six, with all of that length in the hood.

The new straight-engine was more than two common four-cylinders mounted end to end, or a Packard six with two additional cylinders. Packard engineer Jesse Vincent and his team created a truly new 357.8-cid straight-eight engine with a bore and stroke 3.375 by 5 in. and a 4.5:1 compression ratio to provide 85 hp. This engine gave top-line Packards more horsepower and fuel mileage plus substantial weight savings over the Twin Six, which it replaced. For trademark Packard smooth-ness, a Lanchester vibration damper was fitted on the front end of the crankshaft and the engine was given four mounting points.

An air tire pump ran off the transmission and the service brake activated rear stoplights. Watson stabilizers were installed front and rear, and front and rear bumpers were standard, as were a Motometer and disc wheels.

Standard Single Eight Packard bodies were essentially the same as the Single Six, but interior trim and upholstery was more luxurious and appointments more elegant. These bodies included a touring, runabout, sedan, limousine, and two coupe. Black remained the standard for fenders and running gear, and above the belt for closed cars. Standard closed bodies were Packard Blue striped with red until December, the striping thereafter Azure Blue. Open cars were a vermillion-striped Dust Proof Gray, with upholstery in hand crushed brown Spanish leather.

After much hype, 1924 proved to be a disappointing sales year. Packard laid off 2,000 employees at the end of summer 1924; as in the rest of the industry, the quantity of new cars the company built exceeded the number of buyers. By the final tally, 15,067 Packards were built in the 1924 calendar year. That's still impressive, considering prices ranged from $3,650 to $4,950 when a new Ford sold for around $500, depending on the model.

Story and photos by Brian Earnest

HIGH & MIGHTY
After 75 years, stately Packard limo is still a stunner

Except for its paint, Andrea and Ken Chartiers' coachbuilt 1925 Packard limousine is all original.

Sometimes, when in doubt, just go big.

That was certainly the strategy Ken Chartier subscribed to when he entered the car hobby back in 2004. Chartier admits he'd never even been in an old car when he took possession of his amazing 1925 Packard limousine. When it came to the old car hobby, Chartier was as green as the paint on his new Packard.

But Chartier trusted his own instincts, and he really trusted his brother, who helped

him locate the car and helped seal the deal that has pulled Ken and his wife Andrea into the big and wonderful world of old cars.

"It arrived late on a Saturday night and my first time ever even sitting in an old car was the night it showed up," Chartier said. "I got into the hobby through my brother. His passion is old cars. He goes to all the

A pair of folding jumpseats allowed for second-row seating. The clever arrangement is not unlike that found in many minivans of today.

antique auto museums he can find, all the car shows … About five years ago he met a neighbor of his that had a collection of about half a dozen antique cars and through that neighbor he bought a car — a 1931 Chevrolet — and he started calling me up and telling me all the fun he was having with his car.

"That really sparked my interest, and one day I asked my brother if his neighbor had any other cars. I didn't know at the time that he had this collection, and he said, as a matter of fact, that he had a bout half a dozen others. I said, "Gee, do you think he'd be interested in selling another one?" So he checked it out for me and he also had this 1925 Packard."

Chartier eventually traveled from his home

The driver's area is separated by a roll-up privacy window behind the front seat, which. The Holbrook-bodied limousine featured four front-opening doors and seating for seven people.

in Plover, Wis., to New Hampshire to visit the car. A few months later, he swallowed hard and wrote a check for his 4,900-lb., seven-passenger, coach-built new toy. One of the first orders of business when the car arrived: finding out if it would actually fit in the couple's garage. "It does, just barely," Chartier said. "It's 80 inches tall, and it has about an inch of clearance. And it's about 17 feet long, but I'd have to measure it exactly."

Even in the high-fashion, high-society world of 1920s Packards, a jumbo-sized Series 243 limo was not your ordinary luxury car. At the time, Packard was beginning to offer its customers the option of getting custom coachwork on their cars, and an unknown buyer in New Hampshire took the Chartiers' car to Holbrook Company of Hudson N.Y. During the 1910s and '20s,

Holbrook did coachwork for a number of the big players in the world of high-end cars, including Duesenberg, Cadillac, Pierce-Arrow, Rolls-Royce, Marmon, Mercer and Packard. Holbrook was known mainly for turning out conservative, traditional town cars and limousines, and that's exactly what they delivered with the Chartiers' stately Packard.

"I'm the fourth owner," Chartier said. "It was part of an estate in Lebanon, New Hampshire. I haven't been able to learn any more than that yet. The second owner bought the car in 1957. He was an auto mechanic and I've actually talked to him. He was telling me how he repainted it in 1960, but other than that not much has been done with the car. ... The third owner was my brother's neighbor. He bought the car in 1987, and I bought it in 2004."

The Packard still carries its original 348-cid straight eight engine, which has pulled the car through all of its 65,000 miles. The engines were rated at 85 hp.

The luxury Packard began life as a 143-inch chassis and was transformed into Style No. 2711, a seven-passenger "Inside Drive Limousine." The body consists of custom aluminum coachwork over a wooden frame. The traditional boxy passenger compartment is adorned with copious amounts of glass — three large windows on each side, plus a unique tip-out windshield.

All Packards were considered luxurious inside, but the limousines took it a step further. Passengers in these cars were meant to be chauffeured, not just driven around.

"It's got the roll-down privacy window [behind the driver], of course," Chartier said. "It's got a Dictaphone that allows you to talk to the driver. It's just a one-way mi-crophone that's electronic, so you can contact the driver. Sadly, the cable has snapped and retracted into the wall, so it doesn't work at the moment. I need to pull that apart and reattach that and then I think it should work just fine.

"It has a cigar lighter, and a letter box in the back. It has a coat rail for your coats. It comes with a footrest, and comes with two jumpseats in the back, and privacy curtains all around."

As far as Chartier can tell, everything in the plush interior is original. The original privacy curtains are still neatly tied up. The cloth upholstery in the back passenger area is in amazing condition, and the leather driver's seat, while cracked and showing its

A letter hold (top left) was mounted above the mouthpiece for the dictaphone. The intercom-like setup allowed passengers in back to talk to the driver through a funnel-like speaker in the cab (right).

age, has no rips or splits. "I work hard to preserve everything," Chartier said. "You are starting to see some wear on the 85-year-old interior — on the Spanish leather front seat. I've talked to some restorers about getting the front seat fixed and they say, 'Why would you ever want to?'"

That means this is one Packard that is going to stay in original condition indefinitely, with the exception of the paint. According to what Chartier was able to find out from the second owner, the main body of the car was repainted its original green in 1960 and given hand-painted tan pinstriping. Chartier has had the black fenders and

green disc wheels repainted already, and he concedes that he will eventually do the same thing with the green body — which has a few chips and scrapes on the doors.

"They did repaint it in 1960, and I had the wheels repainted back in 2004 and had the fenders repainted in 2005," he said. "But that's about all that's ever been done to the car. The previous owners, if something broke, they'd fix it, but as near as I can tell everything on it is original.

"I'm gonna repaint it. If it still had the 1925 paint job, I might think about [keeping it original], and I hate to lose the hand-done pinstriping, but I'd like it looking new, or with a nicer paint job."

So far, the biggest repair or maintenance project on the Packard has been to the front mechanical brakes. Chartier said he drove the car for quite a while before discovering that the front brakes were providing little or no stopping power. "It turns out the bushings were shot on the front brakes," he said. "So we re-did the brakes on the car. Now it stops much better."

He also installed a set of rear turn signal lights for safety sake. "I found that people just aren't used to seeing hand signals," he said. "I'd stick my hand out the window to turn, and people think I'm waving to them. When I'm at a car show I'll pull those off."

Chartier doesn't believe the Packard's 358-cid straight-eight engine has ever been apart, and even after 65,000 miles, it doesn't appear to be in need of an overhaul. When he first got the limousine, the engine wasn't running right, but with the help of a friend it wasn't long before the Packard was purring. "We actually had to push it out of the [delivery] truck and into the driveway," Chartier recalled. "A neighbor had an SUV and we used that to push it.

"What happened was it had a leaky carburetor float. The float had filled up with gas and sank … The choke was stuck, and the points weren't working right, so they had to be filed down.

"But now, I say it's like a lawnmower. It always starts up, and it always runs."

The car has been running so well, in fact, that the couple were convinced to take their first lengthy road trip in the Packard last summer to show the car at the Milwaukee Masterpiece concourse event in Milwaukee, Wis. The mammoth Packard completed the 382-mile round trip with no problems.

"I was nervous about taking it that far," Chartier said. "My first thought when we got the invitation was, 'There is no way I can drive this car that kind of distance.'

"But we went for it. We took it on back roads, mostly, and Andrea followed me in our Toyota Prius. We got 9.9 miles to the gallon in the Packard, and we got 71.7 miles per gallon in the Prius!"

There were no other 1925 Packard limousines with Holbrook custom bodies at the Milwaukee Masterpiece, and Chartier isn't expecting to see any others in the future, either. From what he can tell, his Packard is the only one of its kind still on the road. "Of the Holbrook body limousines, this is the only one we know of that's left," he said. "The Packard club maintains a roster of all the cars they're aware of and as far as we know this is the only one out there. There are a few other Holbrook-bodied Packards, but this is the only limousine."

One of the nice things about owning an early Packard, the Chartiers have discovered, is the camaraderie and fellowship car owners seem to share. The Packard brand's rich history and loyal following ensures that there are plenty of experts and historians around to provide an invaluable support system. "I've really learned a lot about the Packard company and developed a network

The unique two-piece windshield arrangement has tip-out glass on the bottom to allow fresh are — and probably bugs and dirt — to reach the driver.

of friends that have Packards of this vintage," Ken said. "This car was from New Hampshire, and I'm in Wisconsin, so I really need to get out to New Hampshire to do some more research on the car."

These days, the Chartiers' Packard is a frequent sight on the roads of central Wisconsin. They are definitely not shy about driving the big limousine. "We're always looking for an excuse to take it out," Ken said. "We ask the neighbors if they want to go out for ice cream in it ... And I always drive it for 'Take Your Packard to Work Day' where I work. Of course, I'm the only one with a Packard, but we have seven people in my department, and all seven us can pile into the car and go out to lunch together."

When pressed, Chartier admits that one collector car might not be enough for the couple. It seems likely the hulking limousine will eventually be sharing garage space with a companion. "My brother and I are constantly talking about getting another car," he said with a laugh. "The bug has bitten! He started out with a 1931 Chevrolet, and he just bought a 1925 Moon, and when I talked to him recently, he was thinking about a Pierce-Arrow. And I keep telling me that if he finds one he thinks I'd like, to let me know.

"I'm going to hang onto this one as long as I can. It's just fun! You're up high. Everybody waves at you. Everybody wants to come up and talk to you about the car. It's just a ton of fun."

BORN LEADER

'Firstmanship' was a Packard trademark

Packard firsts were tested at the company's proving grounds near Utica, Mich. This scene from 1932 shows a new sedan connected to the famous Packard Towing Dynamometer, a testing device based on an older sedan.

Packard never seemed to be short of ideas. Since the brand was built from 1899 to 1958, I suppose that says something about success.

Some of those firsts were simple. Most new car buyers would never have thought much of them, while mechanics may have marveled and studied the changes — even chatted with friends about the company's wisdom.

Following are a few examples of self-proclaimed firsts by the Packard Motor Car Co.

■ Packard was first to design and use thermostatically controlled water circulation. Mechanically, it was a big deal, since it meant a car could regulate consistent temperature. That made long hauls, high climbs and fast speeds more reliable. The cars would not be prone to overheating as before. Here's another first: Packard located the hand-brake lever at the driver's left. It doesn't seem like much, but it meant more control for the driver.

■ Packard was first to use a steering wheel as standard equipment and used the

"H" shift pattern on all models. OK, so maybe a few car makers were toying with the steering wheel, but it was Packard that went for it whole-hog. That was a pretty significant step in 1901 when tillers were still being employed by many carmakers. As for the "H," well, time proved Packard right. It became *the* standard!

■ When Packard decided to connect the accelerator pedal to the hand throttle, it was a significant step forward in ease of control. When it made wheels interchangeable at the hub, that, too was big stuff. It meant that wheels could be quickly removed and flats fixed with less hassle, less cost.

■ We don't often use outside luggage racks, but in the 1920s and 1930s they were all the rage for expensive cars, since long tours were in vogue. Again, Packard

was first by patenting a rear rack. Unseen to many people, Packard also patented the present radiator design with top and bottom reservoirs and tubes running between.

■ Packard was the pioneer of the 12-cylinder engine in "V" formation (although the company was pained to call it a V-12, since that smacked of bowing to Cadillac's use of the term V-8). The designation "Packard Twelve" also sounded swankier than "Packard V-12" (at least in the minds of officials). Packard later went on to be the first maker of a 24-cylinder engine (the company loved to tinker with marine and aircraft motors).

Imagine the advantage these firsts — minor or major — for sales. "Yes, sir, Mr. Buyer," says John Q. Salesman. "We have just the car that will serve your needs and preferences." Packard literature, which was usually top-notch in the industry, amply depicted about as much technical detail as most distinguished buyers wanted to know. Views of special advancements and improved features abounded. All it took was a few instructive minutes with John Q. Salesman, and Mr. Buyer was an educated purchaser — in the Packard school of thought.

This wasn't brainwashing, it was truth. Honest revelation, thanks to Packard's ingenuity, business savvy and "firstmanship."

All these first happened before World War II. In fact, way before that war. By 1920, Packard could fan through a substantial list of firsts. That list continued to grow. Even in postwar America, Packard firsts were legendary, although the rate of invention and integrating improvements slowed appreciably due to material shortages, rising costs, waning interest among car buyers who just wanted four-wheeled reliability, plus Packard's corporate laziness. Those postwar innovations and firsts included the Ultramatic transmission, the first automatic transmission developed and produced entirely by an independent automaker and not one of the "Big Three." The Signal-Seeking radio was a first, but only by a few months, since the early Corvette snatched it up, too.

The last big innovation on Packards is still perhaps the best remembered and most impressive: Torsion-Level Suspension, whereby full-torsion bars, front and rear, gave an immensely superior ride and remarkable handling while offering automatic leveling on passenger and trunk loads. That came in 1955, but by then it was too late for any single innovation to save the grand company.

"Firstmanship" kept Packards innovative, trend-setting, ultra-modern, more pleasurable to drive and a touch above its prestigious competitors. But not all the time.

Packard slowed to a mechanical crawl in too many ways in the late 1940s. When rumors of Cadillac's freshly designed and compact V-8 was circulating before introduction on the new 1949 models, Packard held fast to its straight eight. It defended it in an era that felt the old block was too, well, old. Buyers wanted an engine that featured excitement. It made them feel important. Smart. A winner.

So "firstmanship" swung to Cadillac and to other brands. Packard limped into history. But among collectors, it's a fine, time-honored name with a long list of groundbreaking accomplishments.

To learn more about the great Packard marque, check out "Packard: An American Classic Car" at www.ShopOldCarsWeekly.com

WHEN PACKARD PERSEVERED

Times were tough back in 1930, but Packard hung onto its reputation as luxury leader

If annual tree rings are a good gauge of growth, then annual sale results act similarly for the car industry. Among early luxury brands in America, Packard was the dominating force.

In 1930, the cold, hard fact of the matter hadn't quite settled in. While the American public knew there had been a crash on Wall Street in October 1929, the automotive industry kept rolling along for several months at a reduced pace as the economic situation turned into an outright depression.

How well did Packard fare as the favored car of the elite? Let's examine its sales success in May 1930. A leading industry analyst studied sales for all American makes that month. That study included 32 states, plus the District of Columbia. Ford dominated sales with more than 86,200 units. Chevrolet came next with nearly 50,300. There was a dramatic drop to the third-biggest seller, which was Pontiac, at 6,037 cars. Plymouth was fourth at 6,056. Buick was close behind with 5,931.

Other brands that sold 2,000 or more for May 1930 were, in alphabetical order: Chrysler (5,187), De Soto (2,540), Dodge (5,652),

Packard promotional sales literature was varied and downright artistic in many cases. This is the company's official photo of its 1930 pieces, each meant to sell a car!

Essex (5,029), Graham (2,883), Hudson (2,490), Nash (3,456), Oldsmobile (4,225), Studebaker (2,484) and Willys (2,975).

The top part of that list did not include Packard. The prestige car — and that's what every model was for the brand in 1930 — totaled 1,653 units for May. Still, Packard was ahead of more than 18 makes. Offerings for car buyers in 1930 were certainly diverse. The other brands that sold less than Packard were Auburn (just over 800), Blackhawk (with only 20), Cadillac (631), Cord (155), Erskine (a little more than 1,100), Franklin (not even 500), Gardner (125), Jordan (53) and LaSalle (over 880). Pause for a moment and do some calculating. If the Cadillac total is added to LaSalle, it comes to more than 1,510, but still falls

short of Packard's number.

Other makers that fell below Packard's sales success for May of 1930 were Lincoln (only 278), Marmon (812), Peerless (which, at 318 units, was nearing its conclusion), Pierce-Arrow (469), Reo (630), Stutz (which was practically gone with only 27), Windsor (a Moon company afterthought waving good-bye with only 62 units for that month) and another 96 combined under lesser makes.

A few makes fit in the category just above Packard's sales total and below 2,000 sales. These were Hupmobile, Oakland and Whippet. Certain key states were not listed for May, including California, Colorado, Kentucky, Michigan, New Jersey, Tennessee, Texas, Virginia and several others. But at least those reporting gave industry analysts an opportunity to peer into the uncertain future.

Packard's sales record was especially good in the following states that reported: Illinois (284), Pennsylvania (276), Massachusetts (208) and Ohio. Then again, so were most of its competitors. It was a matter of heavy concentrations of people that equated, quite simply, to more orders for new cars. But when compared against price-range competitors in Illinois, Stutz had 7 sales, Peerless counted 26, Pierce-Arrow 46, Lincoln 62, Franklin 87 and Cadillac 111. These brands totaled 339 in Illinois sales for May 1930 against Packard's 284. That meant Packard held more than 45 percent of the fine car market in that state. In a slightly lower range, LaSalle claimed 191, Auburn carried 124, Cord 43 and Blackhawk 5.

Illinois showed 23,036 new car sales for the month in early spring. Of that total, only a small 1.2 percent was claimed by Packard. It clearly was a Ford state with 9,417 sales for May, countered by second-best Chevrolet's 4,739.

If you are looking for rare Packards according to where they sold new, look in Nevada for a 1930 model. Only one sold in May of that year. Two sold in Montana, two in North Dakota, four in Idaho and five in South Dakota.

While Packard unquestionably dominated the fine-car field in 1930, it was far from a megalith among the total scope of car makers. In May 1930, total sales of 209,930 were recorded. Packard's 1,653 meant it claimed almost 8/10 of one percent! And this from the industry leader in high-priced cars!

It really wasn't anything Packard did wrong. It was a combination of a soured economy and a scared car-buying public that tightened its belt against luxury items. What was Packard to do? Keep selling as it was, in hopes that this was a momentary affliction?

That's what some car makers did, and they regretted it too late as their doors were padlocked by creditors. Packard was solvent and had cash reserves. Not all luxury car makers were in fine shape. Cadillac had LaSalle to bolster it and a reasonably healthy General Motors to help it ride the waves of potential disaster. Likewise Lincoln, with buoyancy from Ford. Packard had…itself. No diversity. No safety net. Just good, responsive management and a bunch of creative ideas.

Packard slipped in succeeding years as the Great Depression deepened. But its leaders made plans to reinvent the marque. Soon a new Twin Six, quickly renamed the Packard Twelve, was unveiled. A Light Eight was introduced, but analysts determined the company was losing money on each one sold. (It was that good of a car, being made by a company that just did not know how to — or want to — cut corners on quality.) Packard learned how to survive faster than most, but that's a future topic.

Survival of the fittest? Perhaps. Survival of the smartest? Maybe. Survival of the healthiest and most responsive? Probably.

By Brian Earnest

ONCE BITTEN

1936 Packard One Twenty is love at first sight for new hobbyist

Dennis Frank's first hobby car is a beauty: a nicely restored 1936 Packard 120. The 120s remain highly popular among collectors and were Packard's first medium-priced car when they were introduced in 1935.

Dennis Frank had never been an "official" car hobbyist before, but he had secretly admired many old cars from afar — particularly big 1930s cars that he figured would always be out of his league.

But when the Prophetstown, Ill., resident finally decided to jump into the collector car game, he went "all in" — opting for a lovely restored 1936 Packard 120 touring coupe that has quickly become the neatest toy he's ever owned.

"I always thought, 'Boy, if I could ever find one, I'd love to own one,'" said Frank, who became a Packard owner for the first time earlier this year. "I have always been amazed at the way people have kept and

The 384-cid, 120-hp straight-eight of the 1936 Packard 120.

preserved these cars. I just love this car.

"I was looking for a '49, but I couldn't find one, and then I came across this '36. The guy who owned it lived in Elkhorn, Wis., and from the pictures, it almost looked too good to be true. So I went up and visited him, and when I saw it I couldn't believe it then, either."

According to the story Frank was told, the car had been pulled from a garage in the Chicago area back in the 1980s and eventually received a substantial restoration. The work included new Pale Butter Yellow paint with Hunter Green pinstriping, a new vinyl roof insert, new window glass and rubber, new interior and new rings and bearings in the Packard's original straight-eight engine.

"The odometer has only got about 31,000 miles on it, but there is no way to know if that's original or not," Frank said. "The owners had the motor all rebuilt. The running boards were gone and a lot of other pieces were gone. The only thing that hasn't been restored is the dash. That's all original. The steering wheel was kind of cracked and messed up, so that's been epoxied up.

"He had spent the past 10 or 12 years working on it. He had everything re-chromed and put back on the car. I still need

The unique "Queen's Truck" trunk arrangement featured a spare tire compartment below the regular trunk.

about three pieces to make it all complete. I need to find some bumper guards for the back, and the driver's door handle — somebody made one and it looks almost exactly right, but we still need to find a door handle for it."

Frank's car has one other peculiarity — it was given the unique "Queen's Truck" trunk arrangement. "They call it that because the trunk is on the top and on the bottom there is another door. The spare tire is under there. On normal Packards you open the trunk and the spare tire is right there, but this has another door.

"The people that used to own the car took it go Warren, Ohio, for Packard's 100th anniversary and the people there told them that there were only about five of these in the United States. It's pretty unique."

When Packard introduced the medium-priced 120 series in 1935, however, the company wasn't targeting any queens or other royalty. It was the first time the high-end automaker took a stab at a machine that the average American could actually consider owning. The bottom-tier 120s were definitely not strippers or economy cars, but for less than $1,100, buyers could take home one of seven different '35 Packards, and only the five-passenger convertible sedan and five-passenger touring sedan exceeded $1,100 for 1936. That meant you could actually buy two of the "junior" Packards in 1936 for the price of a single 1400 model — the next tier up in the Packard hierarchy.

This was big news for Packard and an important step in the company's evolution. During the Great Depression, the demand for luxury cars slowed to a trickle, and Packard needed a new, more-affordable offering or risk going out of business. The 120 filled the bill. It was warmly received at the time — more than 55,000 120s were built for 1936 after 25,000 were sold during the car's rookie year — and the 120 remains of a favorite of collectors and car buffs today.

Many Packard fans — back in the 1930s and today — actually preferred the 120 series to the "senior" cars. They were lighter, steered and stopped better, were easier to own and maintain and, in the opinion of some drivers, rode better than the hulking Eights, Super Eights and Twelves.

Frank's touring coupe carried a sticker price of about $1,040 when it rolled off the lot, and for that the lucky buyer got a handsome 3,475-lb. car that carried the standard 384-cid, 120-hp L-head straight-eight, a selective synchromesh transmission, 7 x 16-inch tires riding on a 120-inch wheelbase and hydraulic brakes.

"It's pretty basic," Frank said. "There's no clock in it, just a regular speedometer, ammeter and temperature [gauge], and a glove box. That's it. Oh, and it's got a heater.

"The biggest thing for me is just the way it looks. I love the body style, the headlights… just everything about it".

Frank said he didn't have a show pony in mind when he decided to get a collector car. He wanted a car that would be road-worthy and fun to drive whenever the spirit moved him. After he worked out some initial bugs, the Packard hasn't disappointed.

"It wasn't running too good when I first got it because it had apparently been sitting for awhile. It would run nice and smooth at first, but at about 30 [mph] it would hesitate," he said. "But now I've got it running a lot better, and it runs great down the highway. You just go!

"Of course, with those narrow tires, you gotta be careful because any groove in the road, those wheels can grab and just follow."

Frank says the "dings" and other imperfections that remain on the car don't bother him a bit. In fact, it's the car's little warts that make it the ideal Sunday driver. "Oh, it's got a few things that need to be touched up, but that's what I like about it. It's not in such excellent shape that you can't drive it," he said. "I don't want a car that you put on a trailer and haul around because it's so pristine that you don't want to wreck it.

"For a car that is 74 years old, it's in pretty darn good shape. It's still here, somebody took the time to fix it up and keep it that way, and that's what I plan to do, too."

Story and photos by Gerald Perschbacher

SHOWROOM FRESH
Packard's 'Best Year' lineup re-created in Ohio

Classic lines gracing the front design of 1937 Packards were especially appealing on large senior models, as shown in this sampling from the recent Opus II.

Packard officials were ecstatic with the phenomenal sales success their cars enjoyed for 1937. While notable competitors were waning and falling to the side, Packard gained strength amid the Depression. It was a near-miracle in the car industry. That historic feeling of euphoria was captured in 2009 at the National Packard Museum in Warren, Ohio, as a special invitational Packard showroom for 1937 was featured in conjunction with Warren's 20th anniversary annual Packard meet and the 10th anniversary of the museum's current facility.

The showroom was coordinated by Canadian Art James with assistance from wife Helen. Coined "Opus II," the event recalled the Opus Magnum centennial celebration of Packard held in Warren a decade ago. James coordinated that massive invitational display of 300 or so Packards back then, so it was logical for him to head the recent event.

Showroom Coordinator Art James and National Packard Museum Executive Director Mary Ann Porinchak flank one of their favorite cars at Opus II, a 1937 Super Eight LeBaron town car brought from Texas by Bob Supina.

James chose 1937 since it "was a glorious time for Packard and its best sales year ever; 122,593 finely crafted, responsibly styled, shiny new Packards vanished from showrooms worldwide." He said there were 49 models offered that year. About 40 were located and chosen by invitation to participate in the showroom, encapsulated from the elements in a massive, nearly 80-foot-by-200-foot, metal-framed reusable structure, fully guarded and air-conditioned. The structure was generously underwritten by the Edward A. and Catherine Lozick Foundation.

The showroom truly was a sales event. Owners who accepted the invitation and fielded their 1937s donned yellow jackets to become Packard sales experts for a few days, hawking Packard Sixes and One Twenty models or properly persuading affluent buyers to place their cash on a new Super Eight or Packard Twelve. The slogan borrowed from 1937 was "— Get the Plus of a Packard."

However, sales were simulated. Unlike the first Opus, Opus II allowed every "prospective buyer (to) purchase the Packard of his choice at 1937 prices, with special

Junior and Senior models were grouped logically, per Art James. This was the first time since 1937 that so many body styles from 1937 were methodically gathered in one place. Special banners were displayed through the showroom. These were reproductions of actual Packard ads from 1937, thanks to help from collector Bob Zimmerman.

'Packard Museum Dollars,'" James explained. The museum set up a "banker's table" where visitors to the event could present local receipts dated close to the event. For each local dollar that had been spent, visitors received 10 to 20 Packard dollars with tear-off stubs for gift drawings. When those dollars accumulated, visitors figuratively "kicked tires" with sales experts in the showroom. Hundreds of potential "buyers" flowed through the showroom, glorying in Packard's prestigious past.

Sellers sold the same car over and over, re-creating the frenzied sales climate of 1937. Real owners of a car were credited in a sales competition to win a 1942 Ford truck that had been donated by RM Classic Cars. A 1929 Chevrolet paddy wagon used in a movie was the grand prize, eligible for anyone using Packard dollars to make a car purchase in the showroom.

Trumbull County Tourism Bureau, The Packard Club and Packards International promoted the event as "Packard: The Vision," according to Mary Ann Porinchak, executive director for the museum. Their idea was "to ensure the Packard legacy endures."

Secondary events included area tours, historical presentations on the Packard family, a documentary trip across the country in "Old Pacific II" (a 1903 Model F) conducted by brass-era expert Terry Martin, plus an overview of 1937 Packards by Bob Supina. Video producer Richard Luckin offered a private introductory screening of the soon-to-be-seen PBS documentary "Packard — an American Classic Car."

Technical seminars were also provided. Packards International hosted a luncheon and tour of car collections of Gene Tareshawty and Dan Hanlon, where Packards were prominently displayed. A Saturday all-Packard show attracted about 85 other vehicles, and a cruise-in of all makes the next day attracted nearly double that number.

Cars in the 1937 Packard showroom ranged from Sixes priced less than $800 to a Packard Twelve hearse for $8,000. Making the first "sale" was Charlie Duffield who sold a 120 C convertible coupe at $1,000. Making the final sale was Supina, who "sold" his LeBaron town car for $7,500. Bringing the most 1937s to the event was Mark Hagans, who displayed a 120 CD club sedan, a Twelve club sedan and a Twelve limousine.

More than 5,500 registrants participated in the nearly week-long series of events, according to Yost. Along with spectators and museum members, there were 2,085 paid admissions to see the showroom.

"There's already talk about another Opus," James said. "But let's catch our breath from this one before anything more is said about that!"

For information about the National Packard Museum, visit www.packardmuseum.org or call 330-394-1899.

By Gerald Perschbacher

PAST THE PEAK
Packard Held the Banner High for 1938

Higher front fenders on the 1938 Super Eight presented a challenge to mechanics, who occasionally spent time under Packard hoods in order to maintain superb operation.

Since 1937 was a banner year for Packard in production and sales, officials knew that going into the 1938 production round would be a challenge. However, it was their hope to match or surpass the previous year's momentum.

"For 1938, the Packard Motor Car Company has almost completely redesigned its two lower-priced cars and a long list of detailed improvements is announced for the larger higher-priced Super Eight and

Twelve," stated the official introductory release for 1938.

There was a read-between-the-lines philosophical stance taken by the company at that time: "The Packard Eight becomes the successor to the One Twenty. The name Packard Six is continued for its companion in the lower-priced field."

The Packard Eight (sometimes called Standard Eight by collectors) was last made in 1936. Price-wise, the Super Eight ab-

The Packard Eight for 1938 was really the One Twenty, upgraded in length and girth, making it a bargain for buyers.

sorbed that clientele for 1937. But the name "Eight" returned to the line for 1938, albeit in the medium-priced field where the One Twenty was strongly positioned. For buyers of the old Standard Eight, this was an outright invitation to what had been called the One Twenty.

Equally interesting was the comment about the Packard Six as the One Twenty's "companion" in what amounted to the upper end of the low-priced market. Packard had taken an old page from other carmakers, similar to LaSalle as the companion car to Cadillac, and the short-lived Viking to Oldsmobile and Marquette to Buick.

The company bragged on its "new Packard ride," incorporating "a new spring suspension system for the Six and Eight." Those junior Packards were increased seven inches in wheelbase, resulting in a 122-inch stretch for the Six, 127 inches for the Eight.

While senior versions still catered to wood superstructures, especially for the Twelve, the One Twenty and Six were steel inventions. The public was offered "all-steel bodies with one-piece steel tops and sound insulation with 11 different kinds of noise-deadening material." While fenders were declared to be more streamlined, they really appeared bulbous, in step with the styling trend late in that decade.

Some improvements seemed minor. The radiator fan on the Twelve was 22 inches, "said to be the largest used on any motor car," Packard asserted. Bodies were wider. Senior Packards rode on stately chassis lengths of 127 3/8 inches, 134 3/8, and 139 3/8. The limousine and seven-passenger sedans on a 148-inch wheelbase slipped into the Eight range, although its size hardly made it appear as a junior model.

Top models in the Twelve ranged around $5,000 downward. The Super Eight generally liked the $3,000 level and slightly higher. The Eight seemed contented to be priced above $1,000 which was solidly in the medium-priced range. The Six waded around $1,000.

Max Gilman, vice president and general manager of Packard, set the pole high for 1938. Initially, he had every reason to be positive. "As everyone knows, we brought out a completely new car, a lower-priced Packard, in the model year which began September 1, 1934. During that year, our production exceeded that of the 1934 model year by more than 300 percent. Success with this new car kept mounting and the 1936 model year exceeded 1935 by nearly 100 percent."

He continued: "With still another completely new car, the Packard Six, as a companion for the One Twenty, in the 1937 model year we climbed to still another high record. Our production of 121,101 cars exceeded that of 1936 by more than 100 percent. The increase in the number of Packard cars shipped from our factories in the 1937 model year as compared with 1934, when our shipments were 7,231, was 1,574 percent."

Gilman set the pace for 1938. "During this new model year, we cannot expect to register an increase over 1937 comparable to that of 1937 over 1936. At the present, we have not sufficient plant capacity to build that many cars in a year. We do, however, expect a substantial increase. We believe our 1938 model year production will reach 140,000 cars and we could, if the world's demand for automobiles continues to grow sufficiently, build as many as 170,000." In order to make such sales possible, Gilman pointed to the 35 percent increase in dealer outlets in 1937, boosting the number to more than 2,000 in the United States and Canada. Furthermore, "We now have sales and service facilities in many countries where we never before had representation."

It wasn't the One Twenty and Six that were anticipated to account for all of Packard's success. "An important factor to be considered in reviewing Packard's operations (in 1937) is an important gain we registered in production of our larger more expensive cars," Gilman added. "Although not as spectacular...our volume production with the Super Eight and Twelve exceeded that of the previous model year by a healthy margin of 15 percent. This represented a considerably better increase than that registered by the entire industry for the 12-month period. Important to us also is the fact that Packard registered 47 percent of all the cars sold in the big car field."

That's how the 1937 model run concluded. Hope rang far and wide as the 1938s began rolling from production lines and, in the case of the Twelve, from the hands of automotive artisans.

In the final analysis, the 1938 production flow hit snags. There was stiff sales resistance due to the lingering Great Depression and the mounting threat of a world war that already had engulfed portions of Asia and Africa. Packard was not alone in the dip. General Motors laid off about 30,000 workers on Jan. 1, 1938. For Packard, the reality of the first quarter of 1938 showed sales running two-thirds below the same quarter in 1937, which came to nearly $11 million in revenue compared to $30 million previous. The second quarter continued the slide even though Packard prices were reduced.

Production totals are telling. There were 9,295 Eights from that model run made in calendar year 1938. This compared to 13,329 in the same model run started in 1937. Six production had broken 30,000 units in late 1937 but could not surpass 16,000 for early 1938. From total Super Eight production of 2,478 in the model run, a meager 650 were made in 1938. Of the 566 total Twelves, 157 were constructed in early 1938.

Packard recanted. Fast footwork kept the company solvent. For 1939, the One Twenty designation returned. Company officials learned that it wasn't nice to fool with public impressions, which had been confused with the switch in nomenclature from One Twenty to Packard Eight. Even more telling was the shift for 1939 to a more conservative approach to marketing.

Looking back, 1938 seems a transitional year. It bridged the sales peak of 1937 and trailed to the last prewar boom of the early 1940s. Truly, 1938 was not a banner year, but a year to wave the banner and hope.

Story by John Gunnell

PACKARD SIX VS. PACKARD EIGHT

Just how different were they in 1938?

**The 1938 Packard Six has several differences from the 1938 Eight.
The Sixes different hood louver trim, smooth front and
rear bumpers and a lack of trim on top of the headlamps.**

One of the earliest ads for the 1938 Packard looked like one of the now-popular children's games that show two cartoon panels, one with a few things missing. The old ad showed a dark blue Packard Six on the left and a dark red Packard Eight on the right.

At a glance, the only difference between the two illustrations is that the blue car has bright metal finish only on the short louvers near the forward edge of the hood side panel. The red car has bright finish on the

longer, rearmost louvers, too. In addition, the red car's bullet-shaped headlamp shells carry a chrome strip on the top of them.

Closer study of the drawings reveals that the front fenders on the red car are considerably longer, which means the hood is also longer on that vehicle. This makes perfect sense, since the inline eight has two more cylinders than the inline six.

If you continue to study the advertisements, you'll probably notice a difference in the design of the front bumpers between the two Packards. The dark blue Six has a standard smooth-crowned bumper bar. The dark red Eight has a double-fluted bumper. Though it doesn't show clearly in the illustration, the rear bumpers also have the same design difference.

Because the Eight actually has a longer roof panel, the shape of the windows, though very similar, varies between the two cars. You can tell this by looking at the portions of the interior that show through the windows. You can see a little bit more of the interior in the smaller six-cylinder car.

Despite all these minor differences, the cars share a very similar look; and that was by design. The Great Depression had knocked the stuffings out of luxury car sales and increased the popularity of smaller, more economical six-cylinder cars. However, there was little pride in driving a lesser car, so in the later 1930s, almost all automakers adopted the practice of toning down differences between their cheap cars and their more expensive models.

Some companies that sold sixes and eights made sure that the bigger cars had "Eight" scripts or badges, but left any "Six" identification off the smaller cars. Maybe they thought only your mechanic would know for sure what level of car you were driving,

Actually, both cars shown in the aforementioned advertisement were so-called "non-Senior" Packards. For wealthier clients, Packard offered the impressive Super

Eight and the flagship Twelve. The Packard Six and Eight were aimed at upper-midrange buyers, and advertising copywriters promoted their relationship to their luxury-market cousins.

"Want a pleasant surprise?" asked the copy. "Go to your Packard showroom . . . Step into a new 1938 Packard Six or Packard Eight ... And you'll think you're in the wrong Packard." Another sentence was even more explicit. "You'll think you're in one of the senior Packards, the most expensive Packards."

Both the Six and the Eight grew by seven inches in wheelbase in 1938. The Six had a 115-inch wheelbase in 1937 and a 122-inch wheelbase in 1938. The bulk of the Eights had a 127-inch wheelbase, compared to 120 inches a year earlier. The rarer seven-passenger models — a Touring Sedan and a Touring Limousine — went from a 138-inch stance to 148 inches.

The Packard six-cylinder engine also grew slightly to 245.34 cid, but it kept the same 100-hp rating it had in 1937. The Packard Eight retained a 282.05-cid straight eight with 120 hp. Prices on most models increased about $15-$35 from 1937. The five Six models were priced from $975 to $1,135 and the nine Eights ran from $1,225 to $2,110. These cars competed with Buicks and Chryslers and were really great bargains in 1938.

With their longer new wheelbases, the Packards looked impressive on the road and

The 1938 Packard Eight, formerly the One Twenty series, has longer front fenders than the Six. The hood, roof and running boards are also longer on this car. The cars also have interior differences.

were roomy enough to fit six people inside. Packard said that the "trunks are so enlarged that you can literally carry luggage enough to take your family on a trip from coast to coast."

Longer wheelbases suggested a better ride quality and the Packards also shared a new rear suspension with the world's first opposed shock absorbers and a new transverse stabilizer bar. The new design added up to a gentler ride with "independent suspension" all around. Engineers compared the cars' ride to that of a train on a track. "Sidesway has been reduced," the ad copy claimed. "That means easier handling and greater security."

Packard's all-steel bodies featured all-steel tops and took three years to develop. They created a stronger, tighter, quieter car. They also added to the Packard's easy

upkeep. Packard challenged all other cars when it came to economic care and maintenance. "They're inexpensive to run," claimed the ad copywriters. "And easy to keep in perfect running condition." Packard chassis points needed lubrication only twice a year and the cars had just 16 lubrication points. That sounds like a lot today, but it was a low number in 1938.

Packard called the 1938 Packard Six and Eight the "greatest dollar value in Packard history." As we have seen, the two cars weren't 100 percent identical, but they were both worthy automobiles deserving of the great Packard name.

The 1938 Packard Six has several differences from the 1938 Eight. A close look will reveal different hood louver trim, smooth front and rear bumpers and a lack of trim on top of the headlamps.

By Gerald Perschbacher

YOU'RE NEVER TOO OLD FOR A BEAUTIFUL PACKARD

As Vic approached his 100th birthday, he enjoyed seeing Packards of any vintage, including this 1953 Caribbean owned by Richard Muehlmann.

Born in 1910, Vic knew what Packard stood for. As with nearly everyone in America who lived in the glory years of the awe-inspiring brand, he knew it meant quality, often reflected a person's level of achievement and was a downright wonderful car in ride, handling and pep, given its day and its competition.

But Vic was a Ford man through and

through. He adored Model T's, liked Model A's and respected anything Henry Ford turned out or that son Edsel Ford dreamt to make. Vic collected Model T's, amassed parts to sell and advised restorers how to get their T up and running. Even into old age, Vic was a major proponent for Model T's. But, truth be known, Vic had a hankering for Packard.

Packard's Six and Eight (One-Twenty) for 1939 were selected as "beauty winners" in a national survey. The car company made good advantage of that unbiased result.

A beauty pageant winner

In 1939, Packard was voted as America's best-looking car. It was not a stunt or a public relations gimmick. Packard made a point about this in its advertisements. "Unbiased survey polls public opinion on 1939 cars and Packard wins the beauty crown." The organization behind the survey was Facts Inc., "not connected with any motor car," said Packard execs. The automaker emphasized that "the survey used the methods of Dr. George Gallup and was checked by this famous election forecaster." Involved in the survey were male and female motorists from one coast to the other.

This wasn't a survey on performance, price or luxury appointments. It was based on good looks. As Packard explained in 1939, "In a personal interview, the motorist saw photographs of all 1939 American cars, taken from identical angles, with all nameplates removed." Each motorist then voted on the basis of a simple question: "Which car do you consider most beautiful?"

Packard did not say how many motorists were interviewed. For company officials,

Unbiased Survey
polls public opinion on 1939 cars,
and
PACKARD WINS BEAUTY CROWN!

that was beside the point: "Many motor cars claim beauty, but this survey shows what the public thinks about it. For 1939, Packard again wears the beauty crown!"

Factory moguls said that Packard stood apart in two major points. One was individualized beauty, since Packard styling was not based on other cars. Second, its beauty was ageless, for "a Packard stays smart, stays looking like a Packard... Not once in 34 years has any new Packard left the owner of a previous model with a 'style orphan.'"

Execs continued: "Handsome is as handsome does — that's a wise proverb. When you buy a Packard you can rest assured it will 'do' handsomely for you. For a Packard is deliberately built to be a better, longer-lived car. It is built, not to the standards of a car in this price class, but to Packard's own standards — and this is said without smugness."

Beauty at a low price

Vic knew all this. Like I said, he lived through the era, saw the ads, heard radio commercials, witnessed publicity events and absorbed car-related news. But Vic never really knew that only $354 down could put him at the wheel of a Packard

Six, maybe even a One-Twenty, which was its slightly more appointed bigger brother. Both were considered "Junior Series" cars, since high-dollar Packards carried a Super-Eight designation or boasted of being a Twelve. Those models, beyond doubt, entered the stratospheric range of the high-priced market in 1939.

Vic probably didn't know that an average trade-in would have been credited for the $354 down payment (about a third of the total price), which meant he could have purchased a new Packard Six "without paying a cent of cash," Packard officials trumpeted. Well, they should have, for that was news in itself!

The Junior 1939 design had its origin in 1938 models, which were all steel in construction and used frames that were seven inches longer than 1937 offerings. This improved the ride over that of the 115-inch platform of the earlier Six. Trunks were larger. Cooling fans were bigger. Independent front suspension augmented handling and ride. A lateral stabilizer helped in sharp turns. The Six delivered 100 hp, 20 fewer than the One-Twenty, 35 fewer than the Super and 75 fewer than the Twelve. But it was serious power, well metered and nicely delivered. Reliable, too.

Owners loved their Packards about as much as Vic loved Model T's. As time progressed, it made Vic wonder: would he, could he, ever buy a Packard?

So it was that Vic became the owner of a 1939 Packard Six coupe. It wasn't new. On that, he had missed the boat. Determined, he found a good original in need of work. It took years to restore, but he did it. Some might say it was a nice little Packard, which it was when compared against its stable mates. But not Vic. "Man, oh man, that Packard is some car," he would say while holding a broad smile. The twinkle in his eye betrayed his inner feeling that ran much, much deeper for the marque.

Vic never gave up his appreciation and adoration for Model T Fords. But until his final day, he kept a prized spot for his Packard coupe, black and shiny, cute yet business-like, just the right blend of styling, performance, comfort and pride.

Vic lived to be nearly 100. A few months shy of that milestone, he slipped away peacefully. But if he were still alive and if "Ask the Man Who Owns One" were still the motto for new Packards built today, Vic would have been first in line to let you know the full story.

By Dr. David O. Hutchinson IV

DAD'S DESIRABLE DRIVERS

A man with the mantra: 'I never want to see myself coming around the corner'

Above, this 1940 photograph shows the 1939 Packard Darrin after it had just been purchased by David Osborne Hutchinson III from a Hollywood car dealer. It is shown with Hutchinson's 1936 Auburn Speedster before it burned in a body shop fire. Right, the author, David Osborne Hutchinson IV, and his father in front of their Spanish-style home in St. Petersburg, Fla., in 1946. The elder Hutchinson drove Classic cars daily in the 1930s and 1940s.

My late father, David O. Hutchinson III, was known for owning many true Classic automobiles during the '30s, '40s and early '50s. Many of these Classics were among the most unusual and desirable cars ever created. In a time one could purchase a new Fleetwood Cadillac for less than $3,000, my father chose to pay $4,800 for a '39 Packard Darrin victoria offered by a dealer in Hollywood,

The 1939 Packard Super Eight Darrin is pictured here against the buildings of downtown Miami around 1940 and also with trees as a backdrop in St. Petersburg around 1943. Note the car's external exhaust pipes and how daily use during the war in the St. Petersburg photo was affecting the paint, evident by the lifting paint on the fender skirt.

Calif. This was an astronomical figure for anyone to expend on an automobile just before World War II, when America was still experiencing the devastation of the Depression.

My father was born Jan. 18, 1914, and from an early age, he was an entrepreneur and self-styled individualist. In 1931, at the age of 17, he had two thriving businesses. After the war, he sold his highly successful scrap-iron salvage business, but retained his St. Petersburg, Fla.-based wholesale nursery company, the World's Largest Wholesale Palm Dealer.

My father was a visionary extraordinaire. It made little difference to him if an idea involved his personal dress, a custom speedboat, his Spanish-style home and landscape surroundings or a certain type of business truck; he wanted it to be classy and noticed. Nowhere was this revealed more than in his selection of personal automobiles. It is for this reason I recall my father's exact words stated on numerous occasions: "I never want to see myself coming around the corner."

My father's affinity with exotic custom automobiles started with a unique 1932 purchase. In the '20s and '30s, European countries held a major portion of the custom-bodied auto market. A team on that continent known for radical body lines and rakish curves was an Italian-born twosome who founded Figoni et Falaschi, a coachworks company near Paris. My father located one of the firm's early one-off cars built for a French buyer, which was later sent to America. The car was a Figoni et Falaschi-bodied 1931 Isotta Fraschini with drop-head coachwork. (Recently, this extremely unusual open Classic was offered in a Blackhawk auction.) The Isotta was to be the first rare custom he would own; however, many other recognized Classics would follow. All were either new or less than a year old when they were purchased, and

This factory photo shows one of the 12 Count Alexis de Sakhnoffsky-designed 1940 Nash Ambassador victorias (six were sold and the remaining six were converted back to Ambassadors convertible coupes). One of these cars was owned by David Osborne Hutchinson III, but no photos are known to exist of his car.

all of these special cars were used as daily drivers. In addition to these rare Classics, my father also owned several expensive "production" cars, provided for my mother and grandmother during the years.

Given my father's taste, I rode in several beautiful examples of rolling art daily while growing up in St. Petersburg, Fla. I recall the comments made to my parents and grandmother by those admiring these cars. Whether in a service station or grocery store, while being dropped off at school, or attending a church function, bystanders noticed the cars my family owned. During school reunions in the years that followed, my former classmates have recalled the cars we had with remarkable detail.

I am not old enough to have experienced all of these unusual cars owned by my fa-ther, but those he owned prior to my being old enough to remember were captured in photos or talked about by my father.

An Auburn and a Cord

The first of the seven custom automobiles my father owned following the Isotta Fraschini and before the custom Cadillac period was a '36 Auburn Speedster. Its power came from the supercharged 150-hp, 279.9-cid Lycoming straight-eight. The low-production Speedster sported four massive chrome exhaust pipes exiting from the driver's side hood panel, giving the sleek Auburn the appearance it was moving 100 mph when it was parked. I retain a picture of this Art Deco Classic, taken prior to the 1940 Miami body shop fire where the two-seat Speedster was destroyed.

The author, David Osborne Hutchinson IV, with his father's second Packard Darrin, a 1941 One-Eighty victoria, in 1946. The author rode in this car as a child for close to five years.

The next Classic was a front-wheel-drive '37 Cord Phaeton with the supercharged V-8. Like the Auburn, this car also had chrome external exhaust pipes exiting from the hood, but in this case, the pipes were located on both side panels. My mother told me this was her car, as it was light yellow with red leather interior and seated four passengers.

The first dance with a Darrin

The first of two Darrin Packards owned by my father was a '39 Hollywood Super Eight Series Custom Darrin victoria (convertible) and was powered by the venerable 160-hp, 356-cid Packard straight-eight. The early Packard Darrins of 1937-'39 were hand built in Hollywood, Calif., by Howard

"Dutch" Darrin's shop on Sunset Boulevard. New Packard One-Twenty and Super Eight coupes were utilized to create the Hollywood Darrins. I have several pictures of this Classic, as well as the story of its original owner and how it arrived in Florida in 1940.

My father had taken the train from St. Petersburg, Fla., to California to purchase the '39, which had been sold by the movie star Chester Morris to a Hollywood dealer. The trip back to Florida was a planned race by my father to see if he could arrive in St. Petersburg before the train. He won by several hours, but slept for two days after that challenge. One has to recall that those were the days before highways bypassed towns. It was something only a young 26-year-old would venture, wanting to prove it could be done in a fancy Packard.

Neat Nash victoria

The fourth custom car was an extremely low-production example. It was a '40 Nash Ambassador convertible hand built by the Russian industrial designer Count Alexis de Sakhnoffsky. Six were built, but only two are known to exist today. I do not have a picture of my father's car, but I do have copies of the original set of drawings made by the Count, as well as my mother's recollections.

My mother recalls my father paid $4,500 to an Orlando, Fla., dealer in 1941, and the car had a small plaque on the dash baring the count's name. I have seen one of the two originals that currently exist, and have spoken to the owner of the other example at his home in Virginia. These six radically customized convertibles were powered by the stock Ambassador straight-eights with dual ignition plugs.

In 1976, my family visited Harrah's 1,100-automobile collection in Reno. My sons and I spent two days viewing what was then the largest single classic auto collection in the world, and Harrah's had the custom Nash there on display. The Sakhnoffsky Nash incorporated certain styling modifications also found in the Darrin Packards: the rakish boat-style windshield, the dropped side belt line and the low-cut doors. It did not have roll up windows, but was like the Auburn Speedster that utilized glass and canvas side curtains. Harrah's example was sold in the early '80s at the estate auction held after Bill Harrah's 1978 death. The other restored example is owned by Reggie Nash of Virginia.

The fifth car I know very little about, other than it was a black '41 Lincoln Continental Cabriolet. 1940 was Lincoln's first production year for this car's Continental European styling. The V-12 Zephyr name was retained in 1940, but dropped in 1941. My father drove it during the early days of the war, including on a trip to Maine to get my mother and me when I was about three years old. I can only imagine how he was able to buy gas for such a trip during the gas-rationing period.

A second dance with a Darrin

The sixth and seventh cars overlapped, as my grandmother and my father owned them during the same period. By 1940, Packard had noticed the successful market "Dutch" Darrin had created with the Hollywood elite for his custom-bodied Packards. The company made arrangements for the 1940 Darrins to be constructed more to their standards, and construction of these cars moved from Dutch's California operation to the old Auburn factory in Connersville, Ind. The 1941 and the last of the 1942 Darrins were built by Dutch, but in a different location. My father's sixth custom, and second Packard Darrin, was a '41 One-Eighty victoria. It was powered by the same 160-hp 356-cid straight-eight engine as the Super

Eight of 1939. This car was off-white with a black convertible top. I have several pictures taken from 1943-1950, as these were the years I rode daily in this spectacular automobile. Some time in late '46 or early '47, my father changed the color to a black body with a white convertible top and a complete black-and-white pigskin interior.

At this point, my father had turned the black '41 Darrin over to my grandmother and sold her 1942 Oldsmobile Ninety-Eight. My grandmother was never pleased with driving the Darrin, as her Olds had been Hydra-Matic-equipped, and she found it extremely difficult to see over the long Packard hood. I recall helping her see around the hood by leaning out my window for a clear view when climbing hills or driveways. "Dutch" Darrin's Packards were given extended hoods by fabricating cowls that placed the rakish windshield further back into the driver's cockpit. This, along with the lower bucket seats and cut-down doors, made driving a challenge for my grandmother. The Darrin was sold in Miami in 1950 to a Chicago collector.

There is an interesting story about what happened to the '41 Darrin after it was sold. In 1989, I attended a regional Antique Automobile Club of America event in St. Petersburg, where many finely restored classic automobiles were being shown. While speaking to the late Tom Mix, the owner of another beautiful '41 One-Eighty Darrin victoria (he was a distant relative of the famous cowboy Tom Mix killed while driving his '37 Cord), there was a burgundy '41 production Packard One-Sixty convertible parked next to him. In the course of relating the story of my father's '39 Darrin and his black '41 Darrin, and how the '41 had been sold in 1950, the owner of the production One-Sixty shared an experience. In 1962, he had been in Chicago to view several Packards for sale by a collector, and among the selection was an original black '41 Darrin with a black-and-white pigskin interior. There was no doubt this was my father's '41 Darrin. He said he could not afford to purchase the Darrin, but did purchase the One-Sixty convertible. He could not tell me where the Darrin went, however, I would like to meet the current owner or speak to anyone who may know of its whereabouts.

A customized Continental

The seventh classic was a '46 Lincoln Continental V-12 Cabriolet, which was purchased in late 1946 or early '47. I do not retain any pictures of the Continental.

My father's Lincoln Continental underwent a radical customizing in either late '47 or early '48. He delivered it to a body shop in Pennsylvania capable of performing the extensive modifications he had designed. The white convertible top, windshield and door windows were chopped or lowered 3 inches. The chopped convertible top, from the back of the front seat to the rear deck or trunk area, was made permanent

Eventually, the colors of the 1941 Packard Darrin were reversed from a white body and black top to a black body and a white top. The author is shown here with his grandmother, Mrs. A.T. Hutchinson, who used the car every day. This circa-1950 photograph was taken just before the car was driven to Miami to be sold. The author notes, "Grandmother was hard on whitewall tires. Remember, the Darrin did not have power steering... I often helped with the wheel when parking."

and non-functioning. Over the front seat area was a matching removable snap-away canvas chauffeur top. At each rear quarter area of the top, my father placed custom oval-shaped portholes, and just to the rear of these were chrome landau bars from a 1926 Buick. The bars were about 16 inches long, and with the oval portholes placed at a slightly forward angle, this car was an astonishing beauty. To top it off, the Continental was painted chartreuse green. The Continental made a trip to California in 1948, when my parents drove it 8,000 miles.

During this era, the Ford Motor Co. placed the smaller Zephyr V-12 engines in these Lincoln Continentals. The underpowered V-12 did not measure up to the venerable Packard and Cadillac eight-cylinder engines. Prior to a 1948 trip to California, the V-12 in my father's Continental had been rebuilt, but he still found the car did not have sufficient power to pull certain Rocky Mountain passes in low gear, adding to overheating and vapor-locking problems that plagued him on the entire trip. In those years, it was very common to see cars carrying extra water in canvas water bags on their bumpers. The pictures from my father's trip are still in my mind's eye, where the Continental had a water bag hanging from the front bumper guard.

After this Lincoln, my father began purchasing Cadillacs, starting him on a new path of expressing his individuality.

By Richard Jansen

PACKERLAND'S PLENTIFUL PACKARD DEALERSHIPS

New Packards line Green Bay's Van-Jansen Motors dealership, circa-1948. The neon sign in the window touts the luxury car maker's famous motto, "Ask the man who owns one."

Sales of Packard motor cars volleyed among several dealerships in the Green Bay, Wis., area from 1921 to 1955. Since there was only one sales outlet for the marque in Green Bay at any given time, the dealerships can be tracked. So upon retiring, I began tracing the story of Packard dealerships in the city. It turned out to be a very short history.

The story starts with A.J. Lucia, who had a bicycle shop in Green Bay, and his brother, Howard, who had a similar shop in Oconto, Wis. They combined forces and formed the Lucia Brothers Motor Car Co. in 1901, and they delivered the first car in Green Bay, a two-cylinder Duryea. Over the years, the brothers handled Buick, Dodge, Duryea, Franklin, Hudson, Pope, Stevens, Thomas Flyer and the Waverly electric.

In 1921, the dealership became the exclusive dealer for Packard, and by 1934, its territory included 12 Wisconsin counties and seven Michigan counties. Despite the brothers' large area, it wasn't big enough to keep them in business through the Depression, so after 1934, the Lucia Brothers dealership was no more.

A different Packard dealership appears in the 1937 Green Bay phone directory. The dealership was Green Bay Motors, and by 1939, it had added the Hudson franchise.

This dealership lasted into the war years before it closed. In May 1948, Van-Jansen Motors obtained the Packard franchise and became the sole Packard distributor for the Green Bay area.

Packards get personal

My father worked for Lucia Brothers Motor Car Co. in its parts department, and eventually worked his way up to heading the department. He then worked in the dealership's sales department before switching to sales at Green Bay Motors from 1936 or '37 until the early '40s. For a short stint between Lucia Brothers Motor Car Co. and Green Bay Motors, he worked for Willard Auto Co., a Pontiac dealer, and St. Johns Motors.

Packard ceased being represented in the Green Bay area sometime during World War II, and so following the war, my father opened Van-Jansen Motors, a Packard dealership, with a partner in 1948.

My dad had been a Four Star Master Salesman for Green Bay Motors from 1937-'40. A strong believer in Packard automobiles, my dad often regaled the family with stories of his sales adventures and the signif-

icance of the Packard in automobile history.

Unfortunately, the Korean War was approaching, so the dealership's tenure was limited to slightly more than one year, but what a year it was for me!

I was just learning to drive when the dealership opened, so cars were very much on my mind, and to have a Packard dealership in the family was truly extraordinary.

One of the pleasures was enjoying the demos my dad brought home. I remember a beautiful blue Packard convertible that I tried to convince him I should take for the evening, but to no avail. Another time, I went to Sturgeon Bay, Wis., to drive back a nice 1946-'47 Plymouth trade-in.

When I was hanging around the garage, he would occasionally ask me to go with an interested party on a test drive. One customer must have had it in for Packard (or Dad), because he deliberately drove the car's wide whitewalls into the curb, not once, but twice!

Early Green Bay dealerships

Dad left the car business for good in late 1949, but his partner stayed on and the business became East-West Motors. But while it was still Van-Jansen Motors, and perhaps afterwards, it was the practice of the Packard factory to ship the cars across Lake Michigan via ferry to Milwaukee, where they would be picked up and driven to Green Bay.

Dad let me drive a car back with him before I had my license, and a Milwaukee

**This ad announced
Van-Jansen Motors' opening.**

motorcycle patrolman drove alongside us long enough to make me painfully aware he was on to us. But then, to my surprise and great relief, he pulled away, rather than pulling us over!

I also recall my dad's partner had an accident while driving a gold Custom two-door on such a trip. The gold paint represented the 50-year anniversary of Packard, and was an impossible color to match. If I recall correctly, the car was painted a different color and became the personal car of the partner.

Don Hutson, of Green Bay Packers football fame, became the next Packard distributor, working under the name Don Hutson Motors. In 1953, the name changed again, this time to Mc Donald Motor Sales. This was the last Packard dealer of record, lasting

approximately into 1955.

Our family purchased our last Packard, a 1955 sedan, from this dealership. The Packard name continued on a Studebaker body in 1957, and production ceased toward the end of 1958, but sales in Green Bay had terminated years before.

Tokens of the past

I purchased a 1950 Packard four-door sedan from the Green Bay Cadillac used car lot in 1965 for $150. It had originally been sold by East-West Motors. A 1948 Packard with a bill of sale from Van-Jansen Motors is also in my possession, as are sedans from 1947, 1950, and 1951, plus a 1947 Packard limousine. Unfortunately, only one of the 1950 sedans and the 1947 sedan are running.

Packards were available through formal dealerships in Green Bay between 1921 and 1955, or for a period of 34 years. I suppose it's fair to say that thanks to Dad, Packards have been a part of our family for more than 70 years, even though the car company survived into '57.

Author's note: Sources for the above information were written remembrances from my father, city directories, the *Green Bay Press-Gazette* (particularly a July, 1934, Progress Edition and a Green Bay Sesquicentennial Edition from August 12, 2004. The city directory was apparently not published through the Depression, and the only phone book available from the late 1930s was for 1937, leaving much to speculation.

PACKARD OPTED TO 'LET GEORGE DO IT' AS A DISTRIBUTOR

Like many downtown dealers, the Berry operation tested the option of new sites in fashionable neighbor-hoods. Even if only to sell used cars.

George was quiet, distinguished, athletic, and energetic. He was the type of man who attracted the attention of officials at the ivy walls of Packard in Detroit. What made him even more likeable was his money, position and contacts.

Born in 1880 in Danbury, Conn., George M. Berry was an Easterner who reflected the best of American gentry. When he entered the car industry with Locomobile around the turn of the century, he boxed with the competition. George wrote most of the advertisements and brochures for the head office. Years later, when Packard officials looked at his credentials, they liked that in the man. He was creative.

However, Locomobile wasn't enough. George had higher hopes. Soon, he was with Willys-Overland, second in command of public relations and a crackerjack writer and promoter, with a fondness for finance. Later, Packard found those qualities to be perfectly suited to its needs.

But George wanted to step away from the hectic pace of corporate halls. He also wanted to be boss. Packard liked that, too!

Why? Packard did not want to hold hands with a bunch of childish outlets in the field.

When 1946 Packards hit the market with fading fenders and stylish lines, many loved it, but production wasn't great due to shortages of raw material after World War II.

Packard wanted men of stellar quality who could establish and maintain distributorships. It was through those strategic locations for automobile distribution that area dealers secured their allotments. Like most carmakers in the first decades of the industry, Packard sold new cars to distributors, who then sold to dealers. This built loyalty. It also took a financial hardship off the factory.

In the early 1920s, Berry learned that Packard had a distribution point open at St. Louis in the central heartland of the county. He bought the business and became a Midwesterner.

In Berry's own words, "Packard represents…nothing but the best," and only the best was acceptable. The building he purchased had special provenance. It had been constructed by O.L. Halsey, the first car dealer in all of St. Louis in 1900 who soon turned to Packard. He, too, was an Easterner who settled in the Midwest looking for business and financial success. As he completed construction of the building in 1914, different duties called him back East, and the point of distribution swung to the Packard Motor Car Co. When Berry came along, Packard knew he was the man the company needed.

"Hundreds of men and women who heretofore have been content with automobiles ranging in price around $1,200 are now Packard Single-Six owners," Berry trumpeted in ads in 1923. "They asked themselves, 'Isn't it sensible to assume that a car as finely built as Packard will give better satisfaction and cost less for maintenance, than any car which frankly does not assume to be built as finely as Packard…?'"

As luxury cars sales went, those Single-Six Packards sold like hotcakes. Berry was flushed with success. Like Caesar, he had come, he had seen, he had conquered. Berry knew there would be more successes. Packard agreed. In the 1920s, the company settled on its magnificent straight-eight engine as the powerplant of choice, although

The towering Berry Motor Car Company still stood tall in 1948. It had been a sales point for Packard since 1914.

the V-12 configuration was resurrected in the early 1930s with a small six also joining the ranks in 1937 beside a lesser eight called the One-Twenty.

George M. Berry proved to Packard that its judgment was sound in signing him on as a distributor. In the company's best years, its distribution points fed between 1,000 and 2,000 dealers, depending on the company's expansion into slightly less-than-luxury lines.

Berry often visited Detroit and seemed to be a regular in the hallowed halls of Packard's elite. Often traveling by train, as did most distributors in the 1920s through early 1940s, he knew Packard presidents on a first-name basis, although you never would have never known it from his proper etiquette. He was just like Packard's top executives: a gentleman's gentleman.

Berry's operation sold between 200 and 600 cars a month. His business also was a direct outlet to the public, so he ran two staffs: one for the dealership, one for the distributorship. The distribution staff calculated the number of cars each of the 70-plus Packard dealerships in the territory should have been able to sell. Based on well-researched estimates, he maintained a solvent business even amid upheavals and uncertainties of economic depression and war.

Packard's best distributors had to be good. The marque could not risk selecting weak, inept distributors that could lose business or tarnish the Packard image. Success had to breed more success. The pedigree of the products were dependent upon its employees' ability and virtues.

It's ironic that many Packard workers were rough-and-tumble blue-collar folk. Many claimed English as their second language. That was OK for the factory, but for outlets relating to the buying public, appearances and finesse were very important. People were not just buying a Packard, they were claiming a piece of the Packard image.

After World War II, Berry knew business would be on the rise in a seller's market where pent-up demand finally broke the dam in peacetime. Unfortunately, the prosperity was all too short for Packard. As with many other distributorships, their once-valued locations became inner-city spots as societal population shifts carried more and more citizens to the suburbs. Few buyers wanted to head downtown for their new car, let alone take it back there for maintenance and repairs.

Some did what George Berry did; they opened secondary outlets in fashionable areas of town. Berry opened a used car lot at a busy intersection, and tried it for a year or two. Meanwhile, Packard and other independent carmakers such as Hudson, Nash, Studebaker, Willys and Kaiser were scrambling for new dealers. Many local repair garages or new businesses launched on a financial shoestring filled the fields of those makers. That did not enhance Packard's reputation, which had been waning since 1947, at best.

Gentleman George Berry knew something was about to happen. The "old guard" among Packard's top leadership had retired, been released or outright quit. Part of the old guard mentality was to preserve those privately owned distributorships. Now that idea just had to go.

That change began shortly after the war. The U.S. car industry generally switched to a direct-zone system, with offices administered by the factory. Packard followed along, and by 1950, had pulled the plug on most of its 75 distributors. Among the handful that remained were Earle C. Anthony (the powerful distributor in California who also served on Packard's board of directors) and Berry Packard in St. Louis.

But the inevitable came and Berry's operation bowed to pressure in late September of 1953. A few new '54 Packards and Clippers (then known as a companion car) speckled the premises as the regional company closed its doors. Dealers were advised to follow the new zone system.

Not all of them did. Loyalty counts for something, noted Avery Green in Paducah, Ky. Years prior, it was Berry who met with him in the street near the shadow of the multi-storied Packard building in Paducah. Berry offered the dealership to Avery, agreeing to finance it if Avery needed the help. Green made it one of Paducah's most successful dealerships, regardless of brand. When word reached Avery of Berry's cancellation, he, too, hung up the key and left the car business after the sale of his last straight-eight.

In 1960, George Berry left this life. But in his heart he was still a Packard man to the end in ideals and manners.

Sometimes, car companies changed faster than their dealer network could accommodate. In Packard's case, that was most certainly true. I'm sure George Berry would agree.

A WOODIE AWAKENS

Original 1941 Packard is back on the road after 40-plus-year slumber

Only 358 Series One Twenty Packard wooden wagons were built for 1941, and few survive. Only eight are registered with the Packard Club Member Directory.

There was more than a little irony at work when Denny and Kim Harms pulled the trigger and bought themselves a rare and stunningly original 1941 Packard One Twnety woodie wagon. The Harms are big woodie fans and run a business restoring old wood-bodied Chryslers, but they wanted nothing to do with restoring this Packard.

Even though they are restorers, they were going to keep their power tools away from this one.

And even though their Packard woodie hadn't run in years — perhaps since the early 1960s — all the Harms had on their minds was getting the car on the road so they could drive it. No more rest for this super-rare pre-

None of the woodwork or paint has been touched on this rare woodie, which has 77,000 miles on its odometer.

war hauler. Even with all its wrinkles and age spots, this was a Packard that was going to get some time on the road.

"I think this is obvious you keep it the way it is," Kim said. "Denny has done a great job with it, he's probably gone over about 95 percent of it mechanically, just made it so we could get in it and drive down the road and have a good time in it, and we have. Since we've had it we've probably driven a couple hundred miles and it's re-ally been trouble free."

"I've been all over the car, and it's 100 percent authentic as far as I'm concerned. Structurally, it's in incredible shape," Denny added. "It's very obvious it has been stored for those past 45-plus years, because those wooden cars wouldn't survive if they had a lot of use and no maintenance."

Fittingly, a car that remains so interest-ing and unusual today has a fascinating and somewhat mysterious past. The Packard came from a large and eclectic collection put together by Don Rook of Mena, Ark. Rook owns and operates a bed and breakfast resort in rural Mena and had been assembling a collection of desirable cars for decades. Among the fleet — which has narrowed considerably after growing to more than One Twenty at one time — were late-1940s Chrysler Town and Countrys, Packards from the 1930s and '40s, and more than 40 Chrysler 300 "Letter Cars" from the late 1950s and early '60s.

The Harms caught wind that Rook was liquidating a good share of collection earlier this year, and when the Packard came up for sale on eBay in May, they couldn't resist. "We started tracking it up until the last two hours, and then we jumped in the bidding at the tail end, and lo and behold, here it sits," Denny said. "We actually flew blind on this one, not having seen it ourselves, but there was a broker involved in doing the eBay auction, and after we bought it we had the post-inspection right that if the car wasn't right they would refund 100 percent of our money.

"But I know a gentleman who had seen the car, and he's a Packard historian, basically, and I called him before I went down to pick up the car. He told me it was a Packard One Twenty, serial No. 5, so it was one of the earliest ones, and in his opinion was one of the only 120 Series woodies that was still untouched — at least that he's known of. I asked him if it was something we could mechanically restore and that Kim and I could enjoy and drive, and he felt it was. That was all we had to hear."

Rook told the Harms he bought the car

in 1966 and eventually had it, and the rest of his collection, shipped from Pennsylvania to Arkansas. His amazing fleet could be viewed by guests at the bed and breakfast, but it wasn't really until the past year that the scope of the collection began circulating in the old car hobby. The vast array of cars were all dust-covered and apparently hadn't been given much attention in recent years, but had at least been in dry storage.

Rook seemingly had a particularly soft spot for his 1941 Packard woodie. When the Harms replaced the old tires on the wagon so they could make the car roadworthy, Rook traveled all the way to their home in northern Illinois to retrieve the old rubber and take a ride in the Packard. "He showed up at our house at about 8:30 on Sunday night, after it was dark," Kim said.

"I asked him if he wanted to go for a ride … So we took him for a ride in the car, and he had the biggest smile on his face."

The One Twenty Series was the second tier in Packard's lineup for 1941 and consisted of eight models. The Harms' Model 1493 eight-passenger station wagon tipped the scales at 3,720 lbs. and carried a base price of $1,466. For that a buyer received a stylish, four-door machine with three rows of seating, some trademark Packard styling refinements and wooden body construction from the cowl to the tail. The options list was short: dual sidemounts, radio, gas heater, spotlight, turn signals, and, believe it or not, air-conditioning.

The Harms' wagon had the optional heater, but not much else. "And we took that out because right now it's full of mud dauber nests," laughed Kim.

"It's got a three-speed with 120 net horsepower, a 282[-cid] straight eight L-head, no overdrive — and they did offer an overdrive," added Denny. "It didn't even have a radio, so whoever bought it didn't go for any accessories."

Production figures from the era can be a bit sketchy, but the consensus is that Packard built 358 One Twenty Series woodie wagons. It's unclear precisely how many remain, but only eight other such vehicles are registered with the Packard Club Member Directory.

The Harms' One Twenty, according to paperwork they received with it, was delivered to Neuhard Garage in Milton, Pa., on Dec. 24, 1940. "Packard apparently pulled their dealership in 1950, but I've already been in contact with the descendants, and the great-grandson still lives in the house next door and he still uses the garage for his personal use," Kim said. "Then we think at one time the car was owned by a woman. I have a box of stuff on the car that I still need to go through. Then we know it was owned by a painter, because you can still see some of the holes on the running boards for a ladder rack. But there are no marks on the top from ladders falling on it or anything... Then (Rook) eventually bought it from somebody in New Jersey. And the story we got was that they had this car in a shed down along a river, and they were going to sell the car and get something fancier, like a [Packard] 180. Well, they pulled this car out of the shed and moved it to another spot, and then the shed with the new car flooded ... but this car was saved!"

The couple figures that the car was pretty much in the same condition when they got it as it was when it dodged a watery death many years ago — minus a layer of Arkansas dust. "I don't really think it's had anything done to it," Dennis aid. "It has the original mats throughout the car, all the original door weltings on it. All original door check straps — with a 70-year-old car you wouldn't think they'd be there. It's definitely been in storage all those years. I question nothing about that. It has 77,000 miles on it, and I have no reason to not believe that. It has the original pistons in it, and the engine had never been apart."

Added Kim: "Nothing is missing from the car. All the beauty strips are on the car. All the trim rings and hubcaps are all on it. It's amazing."

One of the venerable Packard's first big public appearances in many years came at the recent Iola Old Car Show in Iola, Wis., where it turned heads in the Blue Ribbon concours, surrounded by restored and pampered high-end show cars. It was there that the couple got to happily answer a question that was posed to them over and over: "What are you going to do with it?"

"Nothing," said Denny. "We're going to drive it, enjoy and preserve it, with no further restoration."

Story by Brian Earnest
Photos by Kris Kandler

A LONG ROAD BACK

Packard buff gets more than he bargained for with his '41 droptop

Jack Bonham's spectacular 1941 Packard 120 once sat
wrecked and abandoned at the bottom of a ravine.

When Jack Bonham is asked to recount the history of his drop-dead gorgeous 1941 Packard One Twenty convertible coupe, he has two options: The short version, or the long one.

If you are within earshot, and aren't in a hurry, hope that he opts for the long version. It's one of those crazy car tales that is so twisted and convoluted that an abbreviated narrative just won't do.

By the time Bonham, a resident of Shawano, Wis., took possession of the car in 1993, it had been wrecked, abandoned, reclaimed, haphazardly patched back together, shuttled from one owner and one end of the country to another, and fought

81

over in court.

"Yeah, it's quite a story," says Bonham incredulously.

Bonham bought the car from a man in San Francisco after seeing it advertised in *Old Cars Weekly* and elsewhere. "I was intrigued by the car, so I called the owner, and of course, he wanted too much money for it, I thought," Bonham said. "He sent me some pictures, and they didn't look great, but I kept thinking about it.

"About three months went by, I called him again, and he hadn't sold it, and we worked out a price fairly close to the unreasonable price that he wanted."

It didn't take long for Bonham to realize he wasn't going to have a straight-forward fixer-upper on his hands. "I bought it sight unseen. I made the big mistake — I didn't go look at the car," he said. "Had I been knowledgeable on '41 Packards, I could have looked at his pictures and I probably wouldn't have bought the car... I'm laying underneath this car, and looking at the shocks and suspension, and saying, 'This does not look like my book.'"

Bonham wasn't sure he would ever uncover exactly where his car had come from or why it had been so strangely pieced together, but he got a break when he came across a vendor at the annual Packards at Perrysburg event in Ohio. "One of the ven-

dors there was from Tucson, Ariz., and I was telling him about the car, and he said, 'You bought THAT car?'" Bonham recalled.

"Well, the story is, the car tumbled off the road at mile marker four on Mount Lemmon Road, way up high near the ski resort, and tumbled down 250 feet to the bottom of a rocky ravine. Then it was abandoned, and I know somebody must have died, because I know how these doors open and if

you go off a mountain like that, you don't make it …

"So I start digging back, and I find out a fellow eventually came and got it out of the ravine, but he put the body on the wrong chassis. He put it on a '39 chassis … But the guy who had it, he was a dentist named Larry Quirk, he passed away, and the car sat for 20-some years. Eventually, a fellow comes by and sees the car and talks [Quirk's] kids into selling him the car, and he comes and gets the car, goes all around the yard accumulating all these parts that look like they might go with the car, and takes it back to his shop in San Diego, puts it all back together so it looks like a car, and paints it black so it looks old."

From there, the plot gets even thicker. The man in San Diego apparently repre-sented the car falsely as a "barn find" and sold the car to another enthusiast in Santa Barbara, Calif., who in turn peddled it to a lawyer in Montgomery, Ala. "That guy in Alabama was smarter than me and as soon as he saw the car he wanted his money back," Bonham said. "Well, the guy wasn't going to give it to him … so he started su-ing everybody. That was the curse I ran into, because everybody I wanted to talk to about the car was afraid they were going to get sued … But I'm sitting in Shawano, Wis., with all this money in the car plus $1,000 shipping, and I'm not suing anybody …

"Anyway, the only way this lawyer could get rid of the car was to trade it to a fel-low in San Francisco, and that's the fella I bought the car from."

But while knowing the history of his

well-traveled Packard might have made Bonham feel better and made for good story-telling, it didn't do much for his restoration plight. He still had a "Frankenstein" car on his car that "needed everything but a body."

The One Twenty Series occupied Packard's second tier, above the One Ten, but below the One Sixtys and One Eightys. For 1941, the convertible coupe was one of eight body styles offered in the One Twenty line.

The One Twentys carried Packard's straight eight L-head 282-cid mill. The 120-hp engine was mated to a three-speed selective synchromesh transmission with a column shifter. The wheelbase stretched 127 inches and the 15-inch disc wheels were slowed by hydraulic brakes.

The One Ten and One Twenty series for 1941 had a few minor revisions from the previous year, most notably the headlamps, which were sunken farther into the front fenders, and the sidemounts were more hidden on cars so equipped.

The convertible coupes tipped the scales at 3,585 lbs. and came with a base price of about $1,400. Bonham had almost the original sticker price invested just in shipping the car to Wisconsin.

"When I got mine home I was ready to start on an 'easy restoration,' you know, after 25 years in a barn. Then I find I got a nightmare," Bonham admitted. "Then I find out about it going over a mountain and everything … It was unbelievable. It needed everything — a frame, interior, engine, everything.

"But then I found a chassis, in Buzzards Bay, Mass., of all places, and when I bought the chassis I also got the motor,

ting the car painted its factory correct Royal Red, and having a new black top made.

It was impossible to tell what his Packard had originally for options, but "it has every option now!" said Bonham. "It's got the sidemounts, splashers, chrome stone guards. It's got skirts from a '41 LeBaron. It's got the 'K' wheel, the mirror for night driving, the gold feather hood ornament, Packard road and fog lamps, chrome-plated headlight rims."

Today, few could ever suspect the stunning black-and-red Packard had such a disastrous past. Even Bonham has to occasionally pinch himself to make sure the whole odyssey hasn't been a dream. "The scary part is, when you're sitting in the car, cleaning the dash, and you say in your mind, 'I don't believe I own this car!' It's almost a sinking feeling … It's too nice! I can't believe it.'

rear end, shocks — everything I needed! That was just such a super find. Then I had to scrounge a back seat, because it had no back seat. And I needed a trunk lid. And I just met countless people in the search for all these parts. It took years."

Bonham's luck took a turn for the better when he met retired body man David Plattin while taking Plattin's restoration class in Green Bay, Wis. "He still works for friends, part-time and he came to my house one day a week for three years, and he would help me, or I would help him."

Bonham eventually found one last key missing piece, a new passenger side rear quarter panel that could replace the original panel that had taken a beating in the ravine accident, and from that point it was mostly a matter of having a new interior put in, get-

If it hadn't done so already, the car officially came full circle in 2008 when it was awarded First in Class distinction at The Masterpiece d'Elegance in Milwaukee, Wis. At such an event, the '41 droptop was assuredly the only car in attendance that had spent a good portion of its life wrecked at the bottom of a ravine.

Bonham knows one thing for certain: the car's days of bouncing from state to state and owner to owner as an unloved orphan are long gone. "People have asked me if the car is for sale," he says. "I say I think my wife is going to sell it after I go."

50 YEARS OF FACTS

Packard 'came clean' about its past back in '49

The golden anniversary Packard of 1949 carried a magnificent load of history and achievements bourn by the company.

Anniversaries are a time of reflection and, in some cases, "coming clean" about the past. So it was with Packard in April 1949, as the company prepared for its golden anniversary celebration and its 23rd series of cars.

To reflect and "admit," Packard issued a news release. In it were tidbits of information and highlights spanning a half century. Most have been forgotten in the dust of time.

"James W. Packard and George L. Weiss drove an early model Packard car from Warren, Ohio, to Buffalo, New York, in 13 1/2 hours on May 26, 1900," said the head office. A nearly forgotten tidbit followed: The two men "arrived so covered with dirt and oil that the Iroquois, then Buffalo's leading hotel, refused to let them have rooms!"

"Balderdash!" you say? Packard truth, says I.

Countless Packards were vehicles of

privilege. So it was that the company noted, "A Chinese in the Dutch East Indies bought a Packard automobile to drive once a year to visit the grave of his grandfather."

"Fiction, not truth," you say? Packard gospel, says I.

The first mother-and-son team to circumvent the world drove (what else?) a Packard. "Melvin A. Hall, later a noted Air Force officer, as a young man drove his mother around the world in a Packard Six. The trip started in 1911 and was concluded 18 months later in the spring of 1913. The Packard passed through 33 countries, covered 40,000 miles and wore out 117 tires."

Hard to believe, you think? Got to be true, says I.

Some of Packard's claims were a bit, well, "on the edge." The company claimed that the "first filling station for motorists was opened in Los Angeles by Earle C. Anthony, Packard distributor and director, when he entered the automobile business in 1904." It was a little red-and-white filling station and was well known by those colorations.

But the statement may have been edging the truth. Indeed, this might have been the first building in California dedicated to such use. But another claim was made from the Midwest. St. Louis was hyped as being the location for the first building constructed to be a station for gasoline and for automobile servicing exclusively, and that came in 1905. In later years, the news ran

nationally and was agreed upon by petroleum companies. A plaque was dedicated at the site in the early 1950s, then in a matter of months the structure was torn down for progress.

"Packard lied?" you ask. A stretch of facts, says I.

Car companies often tailored select facts to fit their stories. It reminds me of a story from not long ago, when the Soviet Union was a world power. Two cars were entered in a race. One was from Russia, one from the U.S. The American car won the contest. But the Soviets reported: "Our car finished a very strong second. The American car finished next to last." The point is, massaging history to fit the situation and audience is nothing new.

That same Earle C. Anthony spent part of his youth as a car builder. The Packard head office made a point of this in 1949, partly because it was intriguing and partly because Mr. Anthony was a member of its board, and it was nice to please the bigwigs.

Young Mr. Anthony "made his own automobile while a student at Los Angeles High School and has preserved the half-horsepower motor."

"Really?" you ask. No reason to doubt, says I. It was trendy for mechanically adventurous men, young and old, to tinker with the idea of a self-propelled vehicle.

Young Anthony did not enter car manufacturing, but he did dedicate a large portion of his life in the sale and distribution of automobiles — Packard chief among them! Anthony also would enter the radio business, but we have yet to hear that he invented the medium...

Packard's boasts continued: "The oldest Packard dealership in the country is that of Alvin T. Fuller, former governor of Massachusetts. He has been selling Packards in Boston since Dec. 24, 1903." OK, so the company waved the victory flag over Fuller. But there were other dealership locations that could have bragged similar longevity, albeit the local distributorship may have changed hands, but never neglected Packard. One was the Halsey distributorship in St. Louis, which took on Packard in 1903.

But Mr. O.L. Halsey's tenure concluded in 1914 as he moved East to Boston to launch the Dodge distributorship for his brother-in-law, Alvin T. Fuller. Correct! A family connection in two big cities with two big operations handling one of the biggest cars in America. Although Mr. Halsey was very much active with Mr. Fuller, there was no advantage in stating "the whole truth, and nothing but the truth" about the longtime Packard connections.

"Avoidance?" says you. Shrewdness, says I.

What may be most interesting of all the Packard facts issued at its big anniversary was the missed opportunity relating to the trademarked "ox-yoke" radiator design that stamped nearly every Packard in one version or another until 1958 (although versions after 1954 were highly stylized). In 1949, Packard said, "The distinctive Packard radiator lines originated in 1904, five years after the first Packard appeared...." What was missed was a slam against Rolls-Royce! That company's first model was launched in December of 1906. By then, Packard already had a reputation and a renowned radiator to match!

"I didn't know that," says you? It showed the polite side of Packard, says I.

By Gerald Perschbacher

PRESERVING PACKARD'S PROVING GROUNDS

The timing tower of the proving grounds is, perhaps, the most iconic structure of the site.

More than $3.6 million in gifts have been gathered in support of the Packard Proving Grounds historic site. And more is on the way. That's because the effort is a fulfillment of dreams.

The initial dream originated with the Packard Motor Car Co. The company, having originated in Warren, Ohio, in 1899,

and having claimed Detroit as its home since 1903, believed that even its best cars had to pass a rigorous series of tests, unlike ever before. Hence, by 1927, Packard had constructed its grueling proving grounds in Utica, Mich., a casual drive from the factory in downtown Detroit.

The purpose of the proving grounds was

Sitting at the lodge and special buildings at the Packard Proving Grounds in 1954 is this new Packard hardtop.

to destroy a Packard. Only by stretching new and proposed cars to their limits would the company realize their potential for success. By so doing, Packard was among the leaders in refining its products for reliability, performance and durability.

That dream for "quality first" carried over to testing of a different type during World War II. Under lease, the facility provided excruciating tests on battle tanks and tracked vehicles to help win the war. That destroyed the surface of Packard's renown speedway, which then underwent complete renovation when peace returned.

After Packard ceased business, the proving grounds site was operated by Ford. The track was also used for testing innovative

components on trucks. But much of the testing area was no longer used — sand pits, rides over railroad ties, water tests for leakage and buildings with massive freezers to test super-cold conditions.

The dream of Packard glory would not die. When the heart of the old Packard Proving Grounds site was susceptible to destruction under the advance of developers, car collectors banded together to foster a new dream. From this came The Packard Motor Car Foundation and its project to preserve a good portion of the old proving area as an historic site.

"Today's fast-paced, high-tech, fiercely competitive world needs to learn the lessons that the Packard Proving Grounds can

The proving grounds and test track were regularly used in promoting new models, as seen here in 1951. Now, a new a ge of glory may be in store for the aged facility.

teach," explains an official. The non-profit foundation, established in 1997, was successful in receiving 7 acres of land donated by Ford and valued at $1.3 million. By early 2007, more than $1.4 million had been raised in gifts and pledges from individuals and organizations, including various chapters of regional Packard clubs. In-kind gifts (including labor, material and professional services) approached the half-million-dollar mark just a few months ago.

How has the dream changed the site?

Joe Ventimiglia, 21, who has been a product specialist for Kia in Detroit, is proud of his volunteer efforts. He credits his enlistment to Ian MacArthur, a fellow college student. Ian's father is John F. MacArthur, president of the Packard Motor Car Foundation.

"Over the past summers, we've been involved in restoring the Packard timing tower, the lodge and the Chrysler build-

The 2006 Packard Automobile Classics (PAC) club national meet was held at the proving grounds. Club members enjoyed the opportunity to photograph their old Packards on the test track in front of the timing tower. (Craig Handley photo)

ing (used during the war)," says Joe. "We repaint, replace glass, repair pillars, add shingles, bringing them back to the way they used to look. In the lodge, we've been revamping the whole library, the kitchen; during the whole time there are restored cars coming in and out." Individuals have also worked on the old hangar, which was moved to its present location. A good percentage of the test track remains. However, it is not sufficient to test cars as in the glory days of Packard.

This writer can attest to the danger of an old test track. When meets had been held at the site in the 1980s, some old car owners pushed a heavy foot on the accelerator to see if it was true that test drivers could whip through the oval track's curves at 100 mph, remove their hands from the steering wheel and still ride the bend due to the brilliantly engineered qualities of the track. This created potential dangers for slower-moving cars. Now, that danger has been eliminated. Still, if a person ponders the past, the pounding of high-speed tires can almost be heard.

New housing has taken over some of the old test land. The plant and office complex used by Packard and Ford were torn down.

PAC members tour the proving grounds garage and engineering building at the 2006 PAC national meet. (Craig Handley photo)

This 1948 Packard Super Eight convertible, displayed at the proving grounds in front of the lodge, is owned by John MacArthur, president of The Packard Motor Car Foundation. (Craig Handley photo)

Recreational land was also set aside.

In a bygone age, Charles Vincent had been in charge of the Packard Proving Grounds. He was the brother of Packard's chief engineer Jesse Vincent. The two had a running feud, of sorts. It was rumored that Jesse tried to design the cars mechanically, while Charles tried to tear them apart in testing. The competition between the brothers helped strengthen Packard's reputation for quality.

But there is no time even for good-natured feuding among today's volunteers. Work teams tackle the jobs, fixing leaky roofs, redoing doors, landscaping, re-shrubbing according to original pictures and much more. The goal is to return the site to its authentic appearance. In addition to car hobbyists, Ford employees and students have been at work on the project. Within a couple years, the possibility exists to have all interiors revamped and a museum in operation. While many workers are in their 20s, supervision is provided by individuals in step with history and Packard traditions. Everything is checked for accuracy.

Local residents who have a Packard connection or who appreciate the site's history have been fond of the project. Some visit practically every day when work crews are at their peak.

The overall dream now being realized in part has several phases. These include the lodge and lodge garage; turning the repair garage into the event hub of the proving grounds and the engineering building and museum exhibitions. This phase includes a National Arsenal of Democracy Museum in the 20,000-square-foot structure.

Future progress will hinge on many hours of labor and donations, if the dream is to be realized. The museum, with a meeting and banquet facility, is estimated to cost $3 million. Further site acquisition could be another $2.5 million.

A fundraising campaign is now in the works. It involves giving levels from $25,000 to $1 million or more. Large contributors will be considered as Charter Donors of The Packard Society.

"Your gift…will make up the majority of the dollars necessary to make this vision a reality," says an official with the foundation. "This probably is the only remaining site that has the potential to be preserved for future generations. If it is not renovated at this time, chances are…the property will be redeveloped as a residential or commercial site. This represents the best chance to help preserve the Packard legacy into the future."

As this writer sees it, such a center near the site of America's golden age of car production is long overdue. Car clubs and organizations of many types will benefit. History will be preserved. Knowledge and understanding of the past and present will be appreciated. A massive goal will be reached. And the dream will become reality.

By Sharon Korbeck

CONVERTIBLE'S ORIGINAL OWNER IS PACKARD PROUD

Carl Keller is a Packard man, and while driving his 1949 Packard sedan in a local parade in 1951, he spotted a new Packard 250 convertible being driven by the village's Packard dealer and had to have it. The '49 was traded in, and the 1951 convertible has been in his garage ever since.

Over the 54 years Carl Keller has owned his 1951 Packard 250 convertible, he's gotten 35 trophies, tons of accolades, and even a few women!

"I wanted a nice car... and a 'girl catcher,'" Keller said of the sweet ride he has owned since August 31, 1951. And his sleek turquoise convertible has been all that and more for the 80-year-old from Clintonville, Wisconsin.

Keller is pursuing plans to get in *The Guinness Book of World Records* for "longest continual ownership of an automobile." There's some competition afoot, but Keller isn't too concerned.

Keller hails from a Packard family; his first car was a 1936 Packard he "inherited" from his father. But his first new car would

Carl and Fay Keller pose in the 1951 Packard 250 that Carl bought new.

come a little later, when he was single, 24, and still living at home. He made only about $2,000 a year running the family's appliance store, so he had to choose his wheels carefully.

While he could have gotten a new Chevrolet for around $1,200, Keller remained marque loyal. "In 1949, I bought a new Packard four-door sedan," he said. It set him back about $2,100.

"I fell in love with it [and] liked it so much better than anything," he said. That's saying a lot for the car pundits later dismissed as having the style of a bathtub or a "pregnant elephant."

"The only other thing I considered was a Hudson," he said.

"That '49 was terrific!" Keller exclaimed, noting he got around 21 miles to the gallon back then. "I had no intention of buying another car."

But fate shifted when a local Packard dealership featured its new 1951 250 convertible in a village parade. And while Keller drove another Packard in the parade, he became hooked on the turquoise convertible with the curious red interior.

"It was really classy compared to what was around," he recalled. After chatting with the dealer, Keller negotiated a trade on his '49, which had about 30,000 miles on it. The car listed at $3,800; Keller got it for $1,800 plus his trade.

"My mother thought I was nuts," Keller said.

In his 20s, Keller put lots of miles on the Packard. He used to call the car "Annette," after an old girlfriend. But that name went

away after he married Fay in 1957 (Keller credits the car with helping land his wife!). "We used it as a family car until 1969," when he bought a 1967 Dodge and kept the Packard as a back-up. "I always kept it presentable," he said.

While he wasn't planning on becoming a car enthusiast, history has led him down that path. He's a member of the Wisconsin and national Packard clubs and attends many shows, including the Iola Old Car Show (the convertible is part of the Blue Ribbon showcase). In addition to the '51, Keller owns a 1955 Packard Panama hardtop and a 1975 Honda motorcycle.

Today, the '51 has been fully restored; Keller did most of the work himself. It's been repainted about five times, but has now been returned to its original turquoise hue. Although the engine has been replaced, many of the original parts — including the starter — remain.

He completed the four-year restoration in 1999, in time for the Packard centennial in Warren, Ohio, where his car took second place in class. Keller has gone on to win many more trophies with the car.

Today, the Kellers occasionally take out the convertible, although a 1991 Cadillac gets them to the grocery store. And remember the wife he supposedly snagged with that car? "She's gung-ho," he said. "She wants to go to car shows more than I do."

The Kellers have three daughters and a son, but they're not sure where the convertible will be parked after they're gone. "I'd like to have a Packard for each of them," Keller said.

Even though he has owned about a dozen cars in his life, Keller remains Packard proud. And the best part of owning that car for 54 years? "All the praises I get at the old car shows."

TWO-DOOR HARDTOPS COULDN'T SAVE PACKARD

First of the production Packard two-door hardtops was the 1951 Mayfair, which was introduced in February of that year. Its mission was to compete with the Cadillac Coupe deVille.
(Phil Hall collection)

Two ingredients were key to successful domestic automobile sales in the first half of the 1950s: two-door hardtops and overhead-valve V-8s. Manufacturers that offered both as options on one or more models generally did well; those that ignored the trends met resistance.

Case in point: Kaiser-Frazer had neither. Kaiser's cars were gone from the market by mid-year 1955.

A partial case can be made for Packard. It took until the 1955 model year for it to get a modern V-8, and after the 1956 model year, Packard lived on in name only as a modified Studebaker.

This is overly simplified, however, as Packard had other internal problems bringing it down, with or without its new V-8. Besides, it took Pontiac and Plymouth until 1955 to get modern V-8s, and they both went on to great popularity.

Despite the lack of modern V-8, Packard did offer two-door hardtops that, while never big sellers, were timely and stylish,

It took until the 1954 model year for Packard to add a second two-door hardtop to the line, the Clipper Super Panama. Packard was trying to differentiate the lower priced Clipper as a submake at the time. (Phil Hall collection)

and are collectible today.

The first mass production two-door hardtops came in 1949 from Cadillac, Buick, and Oldsmobile. Packard was near the end of its run of its body that dated back to the 1941 Clipper, so modifying it to react quickly to Cadillac was out of the question.

All-new Packards were out in 1951, and at first there were only sedans and a convertible. In spring of 1951, the Mayfair two-door hardtop was added. Following conventional wisdom, it utilized a steel top and convertible side windows.

For timing, the Mayfair fell in the middle of the industry's two-door hardtop introductions. Chrysler, Dodge, DeSoto, Pontiac, and Chevrolet added hardtops to their full-size car lines in 1950. Packard was joined by Hudson, Plymouth, and Ford in 1951. Following in 1952 were Lincoln, Mercury, Nash, Studebaker, and Willys.

The Mayfair hardtop returned for the full 1952 model year, and generated a production run of 4,068 (1951's short run totaled 3,356 cars).

For 1953, there was an attempt to divide the new Packard into junior and senior models, not unlike the successful 110 and 120 series were set apart from the seniors in the 1930s. Thus, the Clipper was now treated as a sub series for the lower-priced offerings.

Siding with the upscale Packards was the 1953 Mayfair. It drew a record 5,150 orders. It was still the only two-door hardtop offered — but not the only two-door hardtop shown in 1953. The Balboa show car hit in late summer, and featured a lower-profile hardtop on a Caribbean convertible body, with a reverse-slanted rear window. And it did attract attention.

For 1954, the last year with straight-

Revised styling, a new V-8 engine, torsion bar suspension and new Constellation nameplate all attracted attention to this 1955 Clipper two-door hardtop for 1955. The model year was the most popular for Packard hardtops with more than 20,000 being built. (Phil Hall collection)

eight L-head power, the Clipper was even more of a line unto itself and got its first hardtop, the Super series Panama. Its production hit 3,618.

Among the senior cars, the Pacific designation replaced the Mayfair. It was not a barnburner, accounting for 1,189 examples. Model year 1954 marked the first downturn in total Packard hardtop sales, despite having two models instead of one.

Packard merged with Studebaker in 1954 to form Studebaker-Packard Corp. It seemed like a good idea at the time, as both makes were struggling, but the takeover contained the seeds of destruction for Packard as a luxury-car manufacturer.

Packard hardtop sales set an all-time record in 1955, thanks to heavily facelifted styling, new V-8 power, and torsion-bar suspension.

There were now two Clipper hardtops,

the Super Panama and Custom Constellation. Both featured radical two-tone paint and trim, much like the rest of the industry. As a result, 7,016 Panamas were made, with the Constellation not far behind at 6,672.

However, the most popular hardtop was the 400 among the senior Packards, drawing a production run of 7,206, which would make it the most popular Packard hardtop of all time. The 400 was upgraded in trim, status, and price from the previous Mayfair and Pacific models.

A second hardtop-based dream car, the 1955 Request, combined essentially a 400 with a traditional vertical grille. It was popular on the show circuit, but not to the level of the 1956 Predictor hardtop, which was not based on a production vehicle, but rather plans for the future.

For 1956, there were a record number of Packard hardtop models — all were two

Last in the line of Packard two-door hardtops was this 1958 model, based on a Studebaker design. For the first time, a Packard hardtop had no model name. It was joined that year by another hardtop, the Packard Hawk. (Phil Hall collection)

doors. Packard was unable to react to the industry trend of new four-door hardtops.

The Clipper lineup started with the Panama and Constellation, but late in the model year gained the Executive hardtop. It was basically a Clipper with big Packard front and side styling. It was the least popular, at 1,031 orders, compared to 3,999 for the Panama and 1,466 for the Constellation.

Upscale, the 400 was joined by the first (and last) Caribbean hardtop, featuring the three-tone paint and fancy trim of the convertible. Only 263 were made. The 400 order book fell by half to 3,224.

Even though styling studies and mockups of the all-new 1957 Packards were shown, it was not to be. Production in Detroit ended with the 1956 models. There were 1957 Packards to satisfy (or try to) dealers with franchise agreements, but the Clippers were upgraded Studebakers, built

in South Bend, Ind. Despite the supercharger being standard equipment, the four-door sedan and wagon were not successful. There are still Packard people today who refuse to call them Packards.

A pair of two-door hardtops did return to the Packard lineup (without the Clipper name) for the 1958 model year — it was less than a grand finale. The Packard Hawk was a different looking version of Studebaker's Golden Hawk. Also available was a two-door hardtop, which, for the first time, did not have its own name. The roof was all-new, rather well done and contrasted with the add-on fins and bulges below the beltline. The new hardtop was built 675 times, the Packard Hawk's tally was 588.

When all the counting was done, 49,521 Packard two-door hardtops were built from 1951-'58. Survivors today are certainly worthy of rescuing and restoring.

Story and photos by Bob Tomaine

PACKING IT IN
Last Packards rolled off the line for 1956 model year

Packard's final effort came in 1956. This Patrician is one of 3,775 built that year.

Even if they don't actually start knockdown, drag-out arguments, mid-1950s Packards often generate strong and unbending opinions.

Packard had had its share of difficulties in the years immediately leading up to that point, and as the world was caving in for the remaining independent automakers, Packard fought well and much of the time appeared to be winning. In 1941, it had launched the stunning Clipper, a smooth and clean design with just a suggestion of European style. The Clipper returned in 1946, and still looked good, even if what

had been futuristic streamlining a few years earlier now seemed perhaps a little dated.

Packard addressed that problem in 1948 with its first new design of the postwar years. Clearly descended from the Clipper, a big difference was the fact that the separate and slightly bulging front and rear fenders were now gone, replaced by a modern, unbroken surface the length of the car. It was, the advertising explained, "designed by the Wizards of 'Ah's!'" Prospective buyers were told to "watch the envious glances – hear the enthusiastic 'Oh's!' and 'Ah's!' – when this sleek, glossy Packard convert-

The 400 and its four-door sibling, the Patrician, were just below the top of the line in 1955. Only the Caribbean was above them.

ible glides up to the curb!"

The 1948-'50 Packards are often sniped at today for their bulbous quality, which is especially interesting given that they sold well in their day with roughly 250,000 cars delivered over the period. Unfortunately, Packard's chief rival had some powerful factors in its favor at that time and the strength of General Motors was only one of Cadillac's advantages. Obviously, there was nothing new about Cadillac having GM's corporate muscle behind it, but there was something very new in 1949 when Cadillac introduced its modern overhead-valve V-8. It really was the wave of the future; everything from its oversquare design to its improved thermal efficiency to its reduced size represented improvement; While those points are tangible, it was also a new engine and that alone was a sales feature.

Packard, on the other hand, chose to stick with the tried and true; its flathead straight eight's smoothness and sheer quality couldn't possibly be criticized, but it was an old design. In-line configurations and flatheads were going away, but Packard wasn't quite ready to do so, and when the 1951 models arrived, their newness was primarily in style. It was "the world premiere of a daring new concept in motor cars!"

The 1951 Packards didn't even hint at the cars they replaced; they offered "functional beauty with … new low-to-the-road styling! New Guide-line fenders! New Horizon-view visibility!" They didn't have V-8s, but Packard refused to shrink from

For 1955, Packard's Caribbean wore three-tone paint and hoodscoops, but more importantly, its new 352-cubic-inch V-8 was capable of 275 hp.

talking about its drivetrain. Citing a "new concept of performance" might have been a stretch, but the straight eight and Ultramatic transmission combined "to give you America's most advanced traffic-and-highway performance — with spectacular new economy!"

The new Packard wasn't anywhere near as radical as the Clipper had been before the war, but it was different enough that more than 100,000 were sold – and that was better than double the previous year's sales. The bad news, though, was that it didn't last; sales fell to 70,000 in 1952, recovered to 90,000 in 1953, and then dropped to just 31,000 in 1954, the final year for the design.

Oddly, some of Packard's advertising in those years seemed uncertain. In 1953, for example, it called itself "America's new choice in the fine-car field!" in a headline while the ad's first sentence explained that "from America's oldest builder of fine automobiles comes a great new car in the quality field — Packard for '53."

If Packard had any doubts about itself, it simply abandoned them for 1955 and let loose with everything it could, beginning with what must be one of the most successful reskinnings in history. What had been a pleasant but distinctly conservative car in 1954 suddenly became modern and flamboyant. From the hooded headlights and the cathedral taillights to the flashy color combinations and abundance of brightwork, it was a new day for Packard. Getting right to the point of owning a luxury car, an ad titled "Creating True Pride of Ownership" explained that "Packard's talent for creative engineering has produced a car calculated to instill genuine pride in the owner and create a bit of envy in those who have not yet experienced the pleasure a Packard can provide."

It wasn't all show; Packard also touted its Torsion-Level Ride and urged the driver to "discover for yourself ... nothing on Earth rides like a Packard." The system relied on torsion bars and an automatic leveling system and Packard wasn't exaggerating when it claimed that it "smoothes the road, levels the load – automatically."

If all that wasn't enough to sway buyers, though, Packard finally had a modern OHV V-8. At 352 cubic inches, it could produce up to 275 hp in the two-four-barrel version that went into the flagship Caribbean. The obvious comparison is Cadillac's Eldorado, where 331 cubic inches provided 270 horsepower. Finally, things seemed to be going right; Packard was again in a position to fight with Cadillac when it came to both performance and style. Its efforts were rewarded with 55,000 sales in 1955, and then everything went wrong. The new engine developed problems that were corrected, but not quickly enough. The public began to wonder whether Packard would survive and answered its own question by buying from the competition. Packard's merger with Studebaker proved to have been a mistake and the company was running out of money.

Still, Packard wasn't completely ready to give up, and for 1956, it freshened its styling with more heavily hooded headlights, a new grille and slightly different taillights. It added a gimmicky push-button electric shifter and its engine now displaced 374 cubic inches and, with two fours, generated 310 horsepower, "the greatest rear-wheel driving force in an American passenger car."

That it hadn't lost sight of its target market was proven in the statement that, "This year, your Packard Dealer invites you to look at Packard in particular. He knows you will find it a new measure of achievement ... both as a luxury automobile and in your way of living."

None of it mattered.

Sales dropped to less than 29,000 and the 1956 models earned the sad distinction of being the final Packards to be built from the ground up as Packards. Those that followed would be retrimmed Studebakers, and after 1958, Packard was gone.

PRIDE & JOY

There may be a better car somewhere than his Packard 400, but Bill LeGall hasn't found it

Bill and Loretta LeGall bought their 1956 Packard 400 back in 1976, and they have had many miles of happy motoring since.

There are plenty of folks around who really dig their old cars. And there are more than a few who are just head-over-heels, crazy nuts about a particular four-wheeled friend.

And then there are guys like Bill Le-Gall.

If there were a town specifically for people who were over-the-top, totally, insanely, madly in love with their cars, LeGall could run for mayor. The genuine, unbridled joy and enthusiasm that gushes out when Le-Gall tries to describe his lovely 1956 Packard 400 is truly contagious. As far as Le-Gall is concerned, there has never been a finer automobile built on this planet. And after hearing his take on the endless virtues of his Persian Aqua 400, it's hard not to be persuaded.

"Every time I use that car I feel like it's the first time," said LeGall, who has become a well-known figure in audiophile circles while running a very successful speaker repair and restoration service out

The 400 were the two-door siblings of the four-door Patricians in the Packard lineup. A total of 3,224 were produced for the 1956 model year.

of his home in Lansdale, Pa. He is a connoisseur of many things, and lives life with a rare zeal. But when it comes to collector cars, he is set in his ways. There is the 1956 Packard 400. And there are all the rest of the cars in the world.

"I can't even put into words my love for this car," he says. "I can't tell you in words how fantastic it is."

It's probably a good thing that LeGall and his wife wound up with their Packard, because they were actually acting a bit like stalkers before the car was theirs. Bill had owned a previous '56 Packard and was in Ohio buying parts for it when he started quizzing the man who ran the business back in 1976. "I asked the vendor, 'You must

know of every one of the finest Packards in the country, don't you? And he said, 'Yes I do.' I said 'Where are they?' And he made a list of six on a yellow pad, and said, 'This is the best one. It's in Coalport, Pa.'"

But the car in question was not on the road. In fact, it was sort of in hiding, and the LeGalls had to go window peeking to find it.

"On our way back to Brooklyn, N.Y., where I used to live, we decided to drive to Coalport, and sure enough there was a Packard dealership building there," he said. "It was called Hegarty Packard. And this vendor of parts in Ohio had said, 'Walk to the back of the building and look through the window in back in the shop area, and

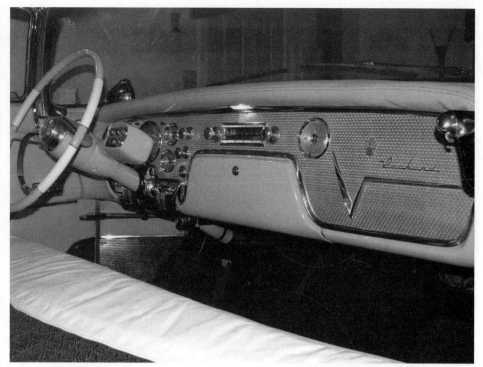

Among the calling cards of the wellappointed interiors on the 400s were the elaborate dash and push-buttom gear selector mounted on the steering column.

you will see the car.'

"Sure enough, we looked in the back window and I almost passed out. The car looked brand new!"

But the LeGalls had shown up on a Sunday and the business was closed. Undeterred, the couple found out where the Hegartys lived and dropped in for a visit.

"We walked down the street there to this home and it turns out they were just pulling out to go to church. I said, 'Are you Mr. Hegarty? I'm interested in buying your '56 Packard.' Well, I had long hair and looked like a hippy, and he didn't even answer me.

He didn't even acknowledge I was there. He just continued out the driveway and took the family to church!"

But the LeGalls didn't give up, and with the help of "a friend who is the smoothest talker in the world," they eventually convinced the man to sell the '56. "We drove back to Coalport, and I brought the money, and I didn't know how he would react seeing me again, but this time he could have not have been any nicer. My friend Morris and I and my wife Loretta spent the entire day getting this car running because it hadn't run since 1960. That's when old

LeGall gave his car a repaint himself in his driveway using original style lacquer paint. He says even show judges have mistaken the paint for original.

man Hegarty had died. He was the original owner of the dealership and it was his personal car. They parked it and never drove it after that."

The trio put in a new battery, changed most of the fluids and somehow managed to get the slumbering car running. Then, against their better judgment, they drove it all the way home in a blizzard, never even turning off the engine that had been silent for 16 years. "It turned out to be one of the two or three biggest snowstorms in my lifetime," Bill said. "And the drive home was over 400 miles ... Mr. Haggerty decided to loan us some skid chains or we'd never make it home. But we made it!"

The lovely 400s were a two-door hardtop subset of the top-of-the-line Patricians. For 1956, a total of 3,224 were produced, compared to 3,775 of their four-door Patrician siblings. Base MSRP of the 400s was $4,190.

Changes in the Packard body, from 1955, included a redesigned grille with a mesh insert with vertical and horizontal chrome bars placed against it. Both the mesh and the grille could also be seen in the "air scoop" opening under the main horizontal bumper bar. Wraparound parking lamps were seen again, but had rounded rear edges. The headlamp hoods were lowered by one inch. Front fenders were extended on all Packards and Executives. Packard hood letters no longer appeared, being replaced by a centrally mounted crest. With the redesigned bumper, the guards were spaced wider apart, placing them directly under the headlamps.

"I can't even put into words my love for this car."

The Patrician sedan and the 400 hardtop both had vertical vents on the rear fenders and the same arrangement of side trim. This consisted of a wide, ribbed chrome band extending the full length of the car between two horizontal rub rails. The first rail ran from the front edge of the upper grille bar to the rear edge of the back fender; the second was parallel to it, about eight inches lower. Both moldings intersected the vent ornament and outside door courtesy/safety lamps were placed at this spot. Also seen on both cars were model identification script, set into the contrast panel, behind the front wheel housing. In addition, both were highlighted by bright metal body underscores that continued across the fender skirts and had wide, ribbed chrome rear extension panels. The Ultramatic transmission offered an electronic push-button selector mounted on the steering column.

The 400s certainly had a lot going for them — style, comfort, reputation and cutting-edge gadgetry. The push-button transmission and air-leveling ride screamed luxury. The 290-horse four-barrel V-8 gave the car plenty of power, and the paint schemes and badging were all top-notch. But as far as LeGall is concerned, it was the car's unique full-length torsion bar suspension that set it apart.

"It has no coil springs or air suspension," he said. "It has a full-length torsion bar, and this thing literally drives like a train. I've had all kinds of cars, driven in all kinds of cars, and I'm absolutely convinced there is not a more satisfying car to drive in my lifetime. It's always totally planted, because it doesn't rely on shock absorbers to keep the car on the ground. The wheels are glued to the ground. You do feel every pebble in the road, and yet you are never jostled. It is the most level ride. It is amazing."

LeGall's car has a full array of amenities, including power windows, seats and antennas, signal-seeking AM radio, dual heaters in the front and rear with separate controls, side running lights and fancy gold plating on the dashboard.

The Packard had 32,000 miles on the odometer when the LeGalls bought it. For a few years, Bill drove it frequently to work. The car now has 99,000 miles.

Bill has tweaked the clutch and transmission several times on his own, and repainted the car himself in the early 1990s. Beyond that, the car is largely original.

"I stripped the car down, I believe in '94, and replaced the rocker panels, mig-welded in new metal to the bottom of the front fenders and couple other spots … And then painted the car using the original nitro-cellulous lacquer, rather than modern paints," he said.

"I had the trunk lid and hood off the car on horses. I painted those pieces outside as well as the bottom part of the car … But the roof I did in our garage. And the paint went on so smooth, it was amazing. It barely needed any buffing at all!"

Not long after he got the car running again, LeGall took it to a show and found out that he apparently had a talent for spraying. "We went to a show in New Hope, and we put the car in the fairgrounds, only so we could picnic behind it. And they announced for your car to be judged make sure your hood is open. My friend Marty said, 'Bill, open the hood. You could win something. I didn't want to do it, but … I opened up the hood, and two or three judges came along, and when they saw the car, they said, "This is all original." I said, 'No, I just painted it. I had pictures in the trunk of me painting it and stripping it.' They simply could not believe that the car was repainted, and that I did it in the driveway. The car took first prize! And the competition was wicked!"

For now, LeGall said he has no plans for the Packard, other than to drive it as much as he can. It will never be for sale, he insists, even though he has had many offers.

He says every "8 or 10 years," he and Loretta drive the car back to Pennsylvania to show it off to the Hegarty family and assure them that the car is alive and well and went to a loving home.

"It's not a show car, it's something I love to drive," he says. "The reason I don't go to car shows hardly at all is that once you get in the car and start driving, you don't want to stop and park it. I'm always sad when I get home and turn the key off and the ride over is over."

Story and photo by Bob Tomaine

A CLIP OFF
THE OLD BLOCK

Packard shuffled the Clipper's status, but none of its positions kept Packard alive

In 1956, the Clipper's grille featured horizontal bars

Few new cars have arrived carrying the kind of baggage and dealing with the level of pressure that accompanied the Clipper in 1956.

Packard was sliding badly by that time, but making Clipper a separate marque as it did that year was no whim. James Nance, Packard's president, took the not-unreasonable position that the company needed a somewhat lesser model in addition to its traditional high-end cars, the trick being that it must not detract from the luxury models' aura. The Clipper began to fill that role in 1953, but its name by then had accumulated considerable history.

The Clipper name had appeared in 1941 on a Packard whose totally new look was distinguished by exotic streamlining that seemed to summon the future. The instantly recognizable Packard grille was there, of course, but it was narrow, and everything behind it was smooth and sleek. The Clipper's fenders and body flowed together as never before on a Packard, and combined with the design's low profile, the car was a standout. Much of what was under the Clipper's skin came from the 120, and while the Clipper was a unique model in 1941, it became a style in 1942 that was expanded to the lower-priced sixes and eights and to the upscale cars. Packard was smart enough, though, to take care of its most conservative customers who might not have been ready for such a jolt; for them, the company still offered Packards that looked like Packards.

Whether change would have moved quickly with the Clipper or deliberately with the traditional models can never be known, since World War II brought an instant halt to the process, but when production of civilian vehicles resumed after the war ended, what had been the flagship Packards at the top of the range were missing, and the entire line instead used the Clipper look. Granted that it was no longer the daring innovation that it had been just a few years earlier, Clipper styling was not something of which Packard needed to be ashamed. Picking up where it had left off with the 1942 models was the industry-wide approach, meaning that Packard hadn't been left behind.

Packard's first postwar restyle was an evolutionary step from the Clipper, one that essentially smoothed and softened the overall lines. Introduced for 1948, it was

well received and counted about 250,000 sales by the time it was replaced with the completely new 1951 design. Unfortunately, style was not enough in those years, as 1949 had seen Cadillac and Oldsmobile introduce modern overhead-valve V-8s while Packard continued to rely on its flathead inline eight. That engine was still in use when the 1951 Packards arrived and completely banished streamlining. Their modern, slabsided design got off to a solid start as first-year sales topped 100,000, but Packard would never again boast of that number. When the company was unable to reach even 70,000 sales for 1952, Nance readied his plan for 1953.

It was simple, the first step being the use of names instead of numbers for all models. Packard had launched the Patrician in 1951 and now, the Clipper was at the bottom and the Caribbean at the top, but the Caribbean was targeted at the Cadillac Eldorado, thus slotting the Patrician against Cadillac's Fleetwood. Some 90,000 sales for the year suggested that the plan had been a good one, but it was not to last.

For 1954, the Clipper moved away from the other Packards with a different look to its tail lamps and quarter panels as sales collapsed to 31,000 cars. What was likely the critical factor was the engine; no one said that Packard's flathead straight-eight was bad, but it was far from modern, and of all the other American cars that year, only Pontiac was still using the same design. And if that wasn't the problem for Packard, there was also the matter of its having gotten another year out of the body that it had introduced for 1951.

The Packard V-8 arrived for 1955 and brought with it a complete restyling. The look was much more modern with hooded headlamps, a finer grille, larger vertical tail lamps and a wraparound windshield. The Clipper retained 1954's rear treatment, which combined with its own trim to set it apart from the other models. Undoubtedly because of the new engine and the new look, Packard sales climbed back to top 55,000 for the year, but since more than 36,000 of those sales were credited to the Clipper, Nance's scheme was not without merit.

Sending Clipper off on its own was the final step, and along with its new identity, it was given new styling at rear and freshened trim. The 352-cid Clipper V-8 was now good for up to 275 hp, the same figure that it had produced in 1955's Caribbean. And although the Clipper was no longer a Packard, it hadn't been stripped of Packard features, such as the Twin Ultramatic transmission, Twin Traction differential and the novel Torsion-Level active suspension.

The split was smart; Packard was now a luxury car and the Clipper was related to it somewhat as LaSalle had been related to Cadillac in the years before World War II. It might have worked, had the rest of Packard's world not been crumbling. One problem was that Packard in 1955 had found itself building its own bodies for the first time in more than a decade as a result of Chrysler's purchase of Briggs, which had been its supplier. Another was the series of bugs — major and minor — that had appeared in the 1955 models. The worst, though, was the tie-up with Studebaker to create Studebaker-Packard Corp. It had been projected as a step toward creating a fourth major automaker by merging with the newly created American Motors, but that never happened, and Studebaker proved to be a less-than-satisfactory partner. With all of that working against it, the Clipper never had a real chance to prove itself; its sales for 1956 were down to a little more than 21,000 and that included about 2,800 examples of the Executive, a Clipper-based model wearing mostly Packard trim and designed to fit between the most expensive Clipper and the least expensive Packard. About 7,500 Packards were sold.

Packard fell off the cliff at the end of 1956, and for the final two years of its production, the company would offer thinly and sometimes oddly disguised Studebakers badged as Packards. The Clipper, though, had something of a last laugh; when it reverted to its status as a Packard in 1957, it also became the only model available and the last to use a Packard model name.

1901 Model C runabout

1902 Model F runabout

1904 Model L runabout

1905 Model N Limousine

1907 Model Thirty roadster

1908 Model Thirty runabout

1909 Model Thirty demi-limousine

1910 Model Thirty runabout

1912 Packard mail truck

1913 Series 2-48 runabout

1913 limousine

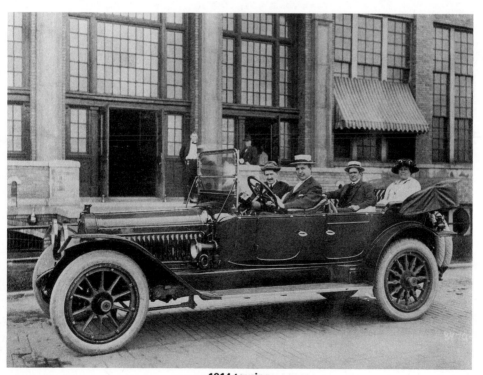

1914 touring

1915 Series 3-38 touring

1916 Seaman body limousine

1920 Twin Six sedan

1924 phaeton

1927 Derham speedster

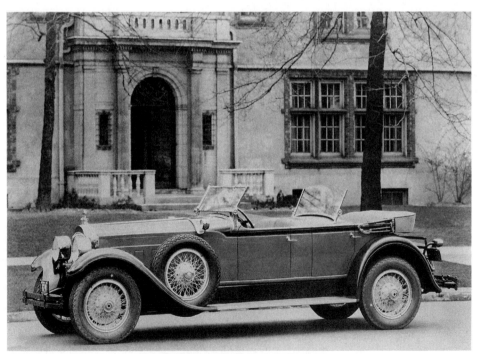

1928 Series 443 dual cowl phaeton

1928 Series 443 phaeton

1929 Series 645 dual cowl phaeton

1930 Series 734 roadster

1932 Twin Six 906 Dietrich convertible sedan

1934 Series 1100 four-door sedan

1934 Super Eight touring

1935 limousine

1935 Cunningham hearse

1937 Super Eight Victoria

1938 Series 1600 four-door touring sedan

1939 Twelve 1707 convertible Victoria

1940 One-Ten 1800 station wagon

1941 One-Ten 1900 convertible coupe

1942 Series One-Eighty Clipper four-door sedan

1946 Clipper four-door sedan

1948 station sedan

1948 prototype two-door sedan

1949 Custom Eight convertible

1952 400 four-door sedan

1953 Patrician 400 four-door sedan

1954 Clipper two-door sedan

1955 400 two-door hardtop

1955 Caribbean convertible

1956 Clipper Super Panama two-door hardtop

1957 Clipper town sedan

1958 station wagon

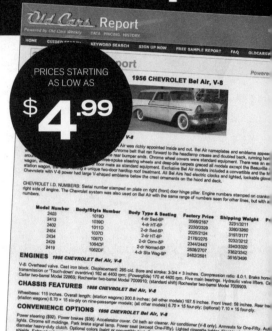

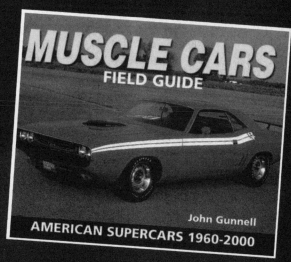

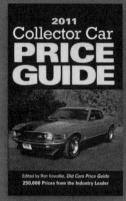
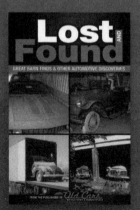
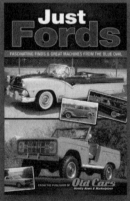